The Fatal Voyage

Peter Aughton was born in Southport but has lived nearly forty years in Bristol. He is a visiting lecturer at the University of the West of England. He is married with two daughters and has two grand-daughters. His previous books include local histories of Southport, Liverpool and Bristol, a biography of Isaac Newton, *Newton's Apple*, and the first published biography of the young astronomer Jeremiah Horrocks, *The Transit of Venus*.

The *Fatal Voyage* is his third book on James Cook. *Endeavour*, describing Cook's first voyage has now been published in five languages and *Resolution*, which relates Cook's second voyage, has recently been published in paperback.

The Fatal Voyage

CAPTAIN COOK'S LAST GREAT JOURNEY

PETER AUGHTON

Interlink Books

An imprint of Interlink Publishing Group, Inc.
Northampton, Massachusetts

First published in 2005 by
INTERLINK BOOKS
An imprint of Interlink Publishing Group, Inc.
46 Crosby Street, Northampton, Massachusetts 01060
www.interlinkbooks.com

Text copyright © Peter Aughton 2005
Maps by John Taylor

Library of Congress Cataloging-in-Publication Data

Aughton, Peter, 1940-
    The fatal voyage : Captain Cook's last great journey / Peter Aughton.
        p. cm.
    Includes bibliographical references and index.
    ISBN 1-56656-610-X (hbk.)
  1. Cook, James, 1728-1779--Travel--Oceania. 2. Explorers--Great
Britain--Biography. 3. Voyages around the world--History--18th century. 4.
Oceania--Discovery and exploration. I. Title.
    G420.C3A892 2005
    910'.9164--dc22

                                                                2005003188

Printed and bound in Great Britain

To order or request our complete catalog,
please call us at 1-800-238-LINK or write to:
INTERLINK PUBLISHING
46 Crosby Street, Northampton, MA 01060-1804
email: info@interlinkbooks.com
www.interlinkbooks.com

To Charlotte Emily

Contents

Illustrations

Portrait of Captain James Cook, 1776 by John Webber *Te Papa, Wellington, New Zealand*

The *Resolution*, a pencil drawing by John Webber *The British Library* Add 17577 f1

'View of Adventure Bay, Van Dieman's Land' by William Ellis *National Maritime Museum, London*

'Cook's reception at Ha'apai, Tonga' by John Webber *The British Library* Add 15513 f8

'A Human Sacrifice in Tahiti' by John Webber *The British Library* Add 15513 f16

'Tahitian Dancing' by John Webber *The British Library* Add 15513 f19

'The Anchorage at Nootka Sound' by John Webber *National Maritime Museum, London*

'King William Sound' by John Webber *The British Library* Add 15514 f8

'Meeting with the Chukchi at St Lawrence Bay' by John Webber *National Maritime Museum, London*

Captain Charles Clerke, 1776 by Nathaniel Dance *Government House, Wellington*

'Kealakekua Bay with the ships at anchor' William Ellis *The National Archives*

'Death of Captain Cook at Kealekekua Bay, 14 February 1779' John Cleveley *Christie's Images Ltd 2005*

A detail from the John Cleveley painting *Christie's Images Ltd 2005*

Maps

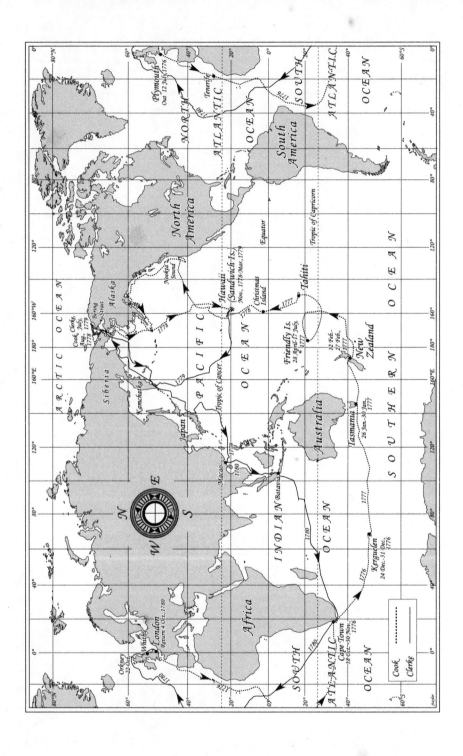

ONE

England

The news that Captain Cook was returning from a second voyage of exploration reached England long before him. There was nobody more delighted than Elizabeth Cook when the *Resolution* docked safely in England after three years of sailing around the world. Sailor's wives were used to sad partings and emotional reunions, but in Elizabeth's case the voyages lasted for several years rather than the customary few months. It was the second time that James Cook had circumnavigated the globe. It was the second time that Elizabeth had suffered the stories of the perils and hardships of navigating unknown waters in uncharted seas. It was the second time she had waited patiently three long years for the return of her husband.

The family was reunited in their home at Mile End. They had two sons now aged twelve and eleven. No sons in the whole of London had more pride in their father's achievements than James and Nathaniel Cook. The father who returned to them was an older man than the one they remembered from three years ago. He must have seemed slightly shorter than they remembered him, but this was an illusion, it was the boys who had grown taller during his absence. His face was more weathered and lined than when he left home. He still had a full head of hair but it was receding at the temples and three years of tropical heat and Antarctic cold had made him much greyer than the last time they saw him. James Cook was forty-seven, Elizabeth was thirty-three and she was still of child-bearing age. Cook's writings add up to millions of words but he never recorded his inner feelings and the personal details of his family. We have no record of his emotional homecoming. What we do know is that soon after James arrived home Elizabeth found she was with child again — it was her sixth confinement. She had every hope that this time the father would be around to see his child grow up.

The admiralty wished to reward James Cook for his services. He was promoted to post captain of the *Kent*, a 74 gun ship of the line which was under repair at the dockyard in Plymouth. The appointment lasted only one day. The next day, 10 August, he was transferred to Greenwich Hospital as fourth captain of that firmly grounded naval establishment. His salary was £230 per annum, with free board and lodgings plus a heating allowance and 14 pence per day 'table money'. Elizabeth must have been well pleased with the arrangement. It gave her financial security for the rest of her life. She could move from the East End of London to the cleaner and more salubrious air of Greenwich. The years of waiting had furnished some reward at long last. Had it not been for the responsibility of bringing up her children she could become a lady of leisure.

One of the tasks which James Cook had set himself was that of writing an account of his circumnavigation of the world with the *Resolution* and *Adventure*. He had recently read the account of his *Endeavour* voyage which had been entrusted to John Hawkesworth during his absence at sea. He was annoyed by the artistic licence and the many inaccuracies of Hawksworth's account, he was dismayed at the fashionable but ponderous Johnsonian prose and he was determined that it should not happen again. What could be a better task for Cook's retirement than to write an account of his second voyage? For a short time all looked very rosy for a cosy family life and a happy retirement at Greenwich.

But there was still a cloud on the horizon. Cook wrote to his old friend John Walker at Whitby in praise of his ship and in reply to an earlier letter. His last sentence betrays his feelings about being pensioned off:

> As I have not now time to draw up an account of such occurrences of the Voyage as I wish to communicate to you, I can only thank you for your obliging letter and kind enquiryes after me during my absence; I must however tell you that the Resolution was found to answer, on all occasions even beyond my expectation and is so little injured by the Voyage that she will soon be sent out again, but I shall not command her, my fate drives me from one extream to a nother a few Months ago the whole Southern hemisphere was hardly big enough for me and now I am going to be confined within the limits of Greenwich Hospital, which are far too small for an active mind like mine, I must however confess it is a fine retreat and a pretty income, but whether I can bring my self to like ease and retirement, time will shew. Mrs Cook joins with me in best respects to you and all your family.[1]

This was not all. In his letter to the admiralty accepting the post at Greenwich he added the words: 'I would on no account be understood to withdraw from that line of service which their Lordships goodness has raised me to, knowing myself capable of ingaging in any duty which they may be pleased to commit to my charge'. He obviously had no intention of sitting back to enjoy a life of ease. He still felt himself to be mentally and physically fit enough for active service.

It is not likely that Elizabeth Cook saw either of these letters, but she must have been aware of her husband's feelings and his restlessness. Even so, further duties in the line of service did not necessarily mean another three years of gallivanting off to the South Seas and around the world. In any case there were no plans for another voyage. Were there? Perhaps there was no cause for concern. Perhaps when he was into his writing and the relaxed routine way of life at Greenwich Hospital he would settle down to his retirement.

There was always the London social round. Cook's achievements, the voyage of the *Endeavour* followed by that of the *Resolution*, had created a great stir in society. People were asking questions about the geography of the world, about the races and cultures of the Pacific Ocean, about New Holland and New Zealand, and about the origins and variety of life itself throughout the planet. The 1768 to 1771 *Endeavour* voyage added the outline of both the islands of New Zealand to the world map, and also the fertile east coast of what became known as Australia. The voyage of the *Resolution* appeared on first impressions to be a less successful voyage than that of the *Endeavour* in that no great new land masses had been discovered. In terms of seamanship and endurance however, the second voyage was even more remarkable than the first. Cook had circumnavigated the Antarctic continent — he had completely destroyed the theory of the great southern continent. He had visited the Tonga Isles, the remote Easter Island, the beautiful Marquesas, the New Hebrides and New Caledonia, he had surveyed and charted many Pacific islands and he had placed them accurately on the map of the world. He had added much new knowledge about the peoples and the culture of the Pacific.

There were a few sceptics. Samuel Johnson, for example, thought that the understanding of the Pacific peoples was far less than the journals claimed, the reason being that the Europeans did not understand the finer points of the language. James Boswell recorded a conversation between himself and the pompous philosopher Doctor Johnson:

> BOSWELL. I gave him an account of a conversation which had passed between me and Captain Cook, the day before, at dinner at Sir John Pringle's; and he was much pleased with the conscientious accuracy of that celebrated circumnavigator, who set me right as to many of the exaggerated accounts given by Dr. Hawkesworth of his voyages. I told him that while I was with the captain, I catched the enthusiasm of curiosity and adventure, and felt a strong inclination to go with him on his next voyage.
> JOHNSON. Why, Sir, a man does feel so, till he considers how very little he can learn from such voyages.
> BOSWELL. But one is carried away with the general grand and indis-

tinct notion of a voyage around the world.

JOHNSON. Yes, Sir, but a man is to guard himself against taking a thing in general. I said I was certain that a great part of what we are told by the travellers to the South Sea must be conjecture, because they had not enough of the language of those countries to understand so much as they have related. Objects falling under the observation of the senses might be clearly known; but every thing intellectual, every thing abstract — politics, morals and religion, must be darkly guessed.

(BOSWELL) Dr. Johnson was of the same opinion. He upon another occasion, when a friend mentioned to him several extraordinary facts, as communicated to him by the circumnavigators, slily observed, 'Sir, I never before knew how much I was respected by these gentlemen; they told me none of these things.'[2]

Both the *Resolution* and her companion vessel the *Adventure*, had taken Pacific islanders on board to travel with them. The *Resolution* took a man called Odiddy and the *Adventure* took Omai. It was not Cook's plan to bring these men back to Britain, he did not feel happy about taking a man out of his own native environment and putting him into the very different setting of a European city. He also remembered his *Endeavour* voyage when the Tahitians Tupia and Tayeto died on their journey from Tahiti to England. Odiddy remained on the *Resolution* for about a year, then Cook returned him back to his own people.

Tobias Furneaux, the captain of the *Adventure*, found his ship separated from the *Resolution* after a terrible storm off the coast of New Zealand. The two ships had been unable to keep a rendezvous at Queen Charlotte Sound. The reason for this failure was the poor seaworthiness and the bad handling of the *Adventure;* she took several weeks working her way into the Cook Straits against strong winds and contrary tides. Furneaux knew that Cook's plan was for another hard and cold voyage to the deep south, following the ice edge of the Antarctic in search of a southern continent. He did not think his men and his ship were equal to the task. When Captain Furneaux realised that he had arrived too late for his rendezvous with Cook he decided that his best option was to make for home.

This was not to say that the voyage of the *Adventure* was a failure. She had sailed the southern limits of the Indian Ocean in a barren quest for the great southern continent. She became the first British vessel to land on the coast of Van Dieman's Land [Tasmania] and she brought back charts and descriptions of the country. Furneaux had wrongly concluded that his landfall in Tasmania was on the Australian mainland and he did not explore far enough to discover that the land was separated from the main continent by the straits which became known as the Bass Straits. The *Adventure* had accompanied Cook's ship on a great sweep around the Pacific Islands when many new islands had been positioned and surveyed. Just before leaving New Zealand Furneaux had suffered a terrible tragedy when twelve of his men were murdered by the Maoris at a place they called Grass Cove. The massacre had left a great cloud of depression over his ship and his crew. This was another reason why *Adventure* abandoned the voyage.

Thus it happened that Tobias Furneaux brought the Tahitian Omai back to England. Everybody referred to Omai as a Tahitian when in fact he was born on the neighbouring island of Huahine, but this was too fine a distinction for an English society which had problems enough getting to grips with the geography of the other side of the planet. It was not the first time that a native of the south seas had been introduced to European society. In 1770 the great French explorer Louis Antoine de Bougainville had brought back the Tahitian Ohutoru to make a great stir at the French court. The English were now able to boast of a similar achievement. It so happened that Omai was the ideal personality to adapt to a new environment and he quickly made himself at ease in London society. A great deal of credit for this must go to the officers of the *Adventure* who befriended him and took great pains to teach him English ways. We must also give credit however, to the botanist Joseph Banks, Cook's gentleman explorer on the *Endeavour* voyage and one of the few people in English society who had actually been to Tahiti. Banks took a personal interest in Omai and he even arranged a meeting for him at Kew Gardens with King George the Third. Omai's greeting to the king was recorded as 'How do King Tosh', this being the best pronunciation the Tahitian could get to the difficult 'g' of the king's name. The anecdote, though amusing enough, is a little unfair on Omai for we shall soon discover that his pronunciation improved very quickly.

> It is very odd, but true, that he can pronounce the th, as in Thank you, & the w, as in well, & yet cannot say G, which he uses a d for. But I now recollect, that in the beginning of a word, as George, he can pronounce it.[3]

At this point we need to introduce James Burney, who sailed with Cook as an able bodied seaman in the *Resolution*, but who came back as first lieutenant of the *Adventure*. He was a young man of twenty-four when he returned from the voyage. It was claimed that Burney spoke Omai's language better than anybody else in England and this was probably true for on the voyage home he spent a lot of time with Omai trying to teach him English. It was thus that Omai befriended the Burney family. With the possible exception of Joseph Banks he could hardly have found a better connected family to introduce him to London society.

The Burneys were a talented family. Dr Charles Burney was a doctor of music, in fact he was the best known musician in London and the most sought after tutor. He was married to Elizabeth Allen with whom he shared two children, but he also had six children by his first wife and Elizabeth had three children from her first husband, making a total of eleven children in the household. When James Burney came home after two years at sea his family had moved from their house at Queen Square in Bloomsbury to a more central location at St Martin's Lane near Leicester Fields, an area which later became known as Leicester Square. They were very proud of their new house for it had a very fine pedigree and it was full of history. Fifty years earlier it had been the London residence of the great scientist Sir Isaac Newton. Doctor

Burney used Newton's study to store his manuscripts. The children played in the observatory at the top of the house, the place where Isaac Newton had studied and measured the stars. The parlour was the room where earlier in the century Newton's beautiful niece, Catherine Barton, entertained the writer Jonathan Swift.

Several of the children were talented musicians so that the soirees in the Newton House were marvellous occasions. Fanny, the second daughter aged twenty-two, had ambitions to become a novelist and she kept a journal which gives us private glimpses into the comings and goings of the family. It is thus through Fanny Burney's diary that we learn about Omai's entry into London society. She describes the scene at the admiralty when Omai was introduced to Joseph Banks. Fanny refers to her brother James by the family name of 'Jem' and also 'Bunny', the latter may have been his nickname conferred by his shipmates:

> Furneaux has brought him [Omai] to Town with him — & he was at the admiralty where my Father had the satisfaction of seeing him. I find myself very curious to have the same sight. He was dressed according to the fashion of his Country, & is a very good looking man — my father says he has quite an interesting Countenance. He appeared to have uncommon spirits, & laughed very heartily many Times. He speaks a few English words — & Capt. Furneaux a few Otaheite words. — They had got Mr Banks there, on purpose to speak with him — but Mr Banks has almost forgot what he knew of that language. But you must know we are very proud to hear that our Jem speaks more Otaheite than any of the ship's Crew. — This Capt. F. told my father, who was Introduced to this stranger, as Jem's Father — he laughed, & shook Hands very cordially, & repeated with great pleasure the name thus Bunny! O! Bunny! immediately knowing who was meant, & the Capt. says that he is very fond of Bunny, who spent great part Of his time in studying the Language with him.[4]

James Burney went to the theatre at Drury Lane with his sister Susan, to see a production of *Isabella* by David Garrick. From their seats in one of the upper boxes whom should they see but Omai in the company of Joseph Banks who was very busy showing off the Tahitian. At the interval James left his seat and went over to speak with his friend Omai. He was received with a hearty shake of the hand and Omai made a space for James to sit by his side. James Burney then asked Joseph Banks if Omai could come to the Burney household for dinner but the offer was rejected. It transpired that Omai was booked up as a guest of Lord Sandwich of the admiralty at Hinchinbrooke, he certainly moved in high circles. The following Tuesday night however, very late, there came a note directed to the Burneys' door. It was written on behalf of Omai. 'Complements to Mr Burney and if it is agreeable and convenient to him, he will do himself the Honour of Dining with Mr Burney to morrow. But if it is not so, Omai will wait upon Mr Burney some other Time that shall suit him better.'

Omai arrived at the appointed time on the appointed day. He had been taken to see the state opening of parliament by George III and he was brought by Joseph Banks and Doctor Solander. Fanny Burney, who was very eager to meet Omai, was unfortunately suffering from a cold. She waited until Banks and Solander had left the house before making her appearance. When she came downstairs Omai was seated in a great chair chatting away to her brother in Tahitian. He rose and he made a very fine bow to Fanny, a gesture which impressed the young lady very much. 'He makes remarkably good bow', she exclaimed. 'Not [just] for him, but for any body, however long under a Dancing Master's care.'

But when Jem went on, & told him that I was not well, he again directly rose, & muttering something of the Fire, in a very polite manner, without speech insisted upon my taking his seat, — & he would not be refused. He then drew his chair next to mine, & looking at me with an expression of pity, said 'very well to morrow—morrow?' — I imagine he meant I hope you will be very well in two or 3 morrows. — & when I shook my Head, he said 'No? O very bad!'—[5]

Omai had been expensively and rather ridiculously clothed by Joseph Banks. He cut an impressive figure in his suit of Manchester velvet lined with white satin. He had lace ruffles and he carried an impressive sword which King George had given to him. Fanny found him tall and well proportioned with a pleasing countenance. He was very polite and attentive and his manners were excellent. Fanny had the pleasure of sitting next to him for dinner, near the fire. Omai was served first, it was his right as a guest of the household, but he offered his portion to Fanny. 'When I declined', said Fanny, 'he had not the over shot polite-ness to offer all around, as I have seen some people do, but took it quietly again.' He discovered from the conversation and the faces, that the joint of beef was undercooked, but he took great pains to assure his hosts that he liked it. 'Very dood, very dood', he said two or three times.

At about six o'clock it was time for Omai to take his leave. He had an appointment with Doctor Solander to see no less than twelve ladies. Fanny thought there must be some mistake but Omai counted them out from one to ten on his fingers and added two more for clarity. Twelve ladies! The remarkable ease with which he entered society was not confined to his relations with Joseph Banks and the Burneys. It is confirmed by James Boswell who recorded some observations of Doctor Johnson:

> He [Samuel Johnson] had been in company with Omai, a native of one of the South Sea Islands, after he had been some time in this country. He was struck with the elegance of his behaviour, and accounted for it thus: 'Sir, he had passed his time, while in England, only on the best company; so that all that he had acquired of our manners was genteel. As proof of this, Sir, Lord Mulgrave and he dined one day at Streatham; they sat with their backs to the light fronting me, so that I could not see distinctly; and there was so little of the savage in Omai, that I was afraid to speak to either, lest I should mistake one for the other.'[6]

It was therefore Omai, as much as anybody, who raised the popular profile of Cook's second voyage in the mind of the public, this was in spite of the fact that Cook himself was still at sea when Omai was making his mark on London society. When Cook returned in July 1775 the Royal Society and the scientific community were eagerly awaiting the findings of his second voyage. Cook's old shipmates from his first voyage, Joseph Banks and Daniel Solander, were eager to meet him again and any differences they may have had from three years previously, about Joseph Banks trying to commandeer the expedition, were soon dispelled. The natural history on the second voyage had been covered by John Rienhold Forster and George Forster, father and son. John Rienhold Forster was not the easiest of men to live with for three years in the confined quarters of a ship as small as the *Resolution*, frictions had arisen between him and James Cook but the natural history had been very well covered.

James Cook was very keen to become a member of the Royal Society and his name appears in the society records as 'Captain James Cook, of Mile-End a gentleman skilful in astronomy, & the successful conductor of two important voyages for the discovery of unknown countries, by which geography and natural history have been greatly advantaged & improved....' He was nominated by Banks and Solander and endorsed by twenty-five signatures and was duly elected. Cook could mix well with the fellows of the Royal Society and could hold his own with the top brass in the navy. His set jaw and impassive manner was ideally suited to the quarter deck of one of His Majesty's ships. It was when it came to mixing with the social and artistic side of society that his personality generated problems.

Cook's first voyage in the *Endeavour* was history. There were still undiscovered islands in that great blue ocean but his second voyage with the *Resolution* and *Adventure* had proved that there were no more great land masses waiting to be discovered. Even in the cold southern latitudes there was no continent, Cook had taken his ship as far south as it was possible for any ship to go. But the voyages had fired the popular imagination. The question on every mind was, would there be a third voyage? There were still many leagues of uncharted coastline in the Pacific. There was also the question of Omai. Popular as he was in London the admiralty felt under some obligation to return him to his people. At some point the North Pacific came under discussion for much of the west coast of North America was still uncharted. But as the discussion developed the main object of the next voyage turned to a quest which was a very old chestnut, even older than the British navy. It was the age-old search for the North West Passage from Atlantic to Pacific. Four centuries of searching from the Atlantic had drawn a complete blank, yet there was still a conviction that the passage existed. With new methods of navigation, with better ships, with the new chronometer and methods of keeping the scurvy at bay, it was now possible to make the search for the North West Passage from the Pacific instead of the Atlantic.

A decision was taken to sponsor the voyage. But what was the best route to take? How long would it take to get to the North Pacific? How long would it take to get from the North Pacific to the Atlantic? What charts were available for the area? Had the Russians made any significant discoveries from their trading posts on the eastern coast of Siberia? They had ships for the voyage. They had volunteers to travel to the Pacific. They had the money for the expedition. But they did not have a commander. It was natural that the admiralty should consult Captain Cook on the preparations for the voyage for nobody had more experience than Cook at sailing a ship in uncharted waters.

It was in February 1776 that Lord Sandwich invited James Cook to dinner at the admiralty in the company of Hugh Palliser, comptroller of the Navy and Sir Philip Stephens, secretary to the admiralty. The purpose of the meeting was to discuss the forthcoming voyage and to ask Cook's opinion on the route, about the choice of ships and many other details. But the most important question was whom should they choose to lead the expedition. It was Cook's first biographer, Andrew Kippis, who described the scene around the dinner table as the four of them became more and more enthused about the voyage. There came a point where Cook could stand it no longer. 'Captain Cook was so fired with the contemplation and representation of the object, that he started up, and declared that he himself would undertake the direction of the enterprise.'[7] The idea that a man as mature and unemotional as James Cook would make such a sudden and momentous decision on the spur of the moment is possibly out of character. There are some who claim that it was the prize of twenty thousand pounds for the discovery of the North West Passage which decided him. Whatever the truth behind the famous dinner party Cook came away with the commission. On 14 February he was writing to his trusted correspondent John Walker at Whitby, his letter is full of typical Cook understatements:

> I should have Answered your last favour sooner, but waited to know whether I should go to Greenwich Hospital, or the South Sea. The latter is now fixed upon; I expect to be ready to sail about the latter end of Ap[ril] with my old ship the Resolution and the Discovery, the ship lately purchased of Mr Herbert. I know not what your opinion may be on this step I have taken. It is certain I have quited an easy retirement, for an Active, and perhaps Dangerous Voyage. My present disposition is more favourable to the latter than the former, and I imbark on as fair a prospect as I can wish. If I am fortunate enough to get safe home, theres no doubt but it will be greatly to my advantage.[8]

The quiet life of Greenwich Hospital was not to his liking. The sea called to him again. He could not resist the lure of the blue skies, the open seas and the white surf of the greatest ocean on the earth. He longed again for the Pacific Islands and their dark skinned chattering peoples. There were new coastlines to be charted and islands still to be added to the map of the world. He longed again for the Pacific swell and the heaving of the ship beneath his feet, the creaking of the timbers and the rustle of the sails in the wind. He longed for the tropical sunsets and the sudden dawn of a new day. But the voyage would not be confined to the warmth of a perpetual summer, he would have to suffer too the bitter cold of the Arctic seas, perhaps even colder than the ice edge cruise of the Antarctic. The prize he wanted more than anything was to be the first man to sail his ship across the north of the American continent.

Yes. Captain Cook had given up an easy retirement in return for another dangerous voyage of exploration. But how did he break the news to his wife? Elizabeth was carrying another child when she heard the news. How did he tell her that she was to be a sailor's widow again for at least another three years? Perhaps he would be gone for more than three years. This time he might not be so lucky, he might never return. James and Elizabeth Cook already had the financial security for which they had worked so hard. James Cook had already done far more for his country than the call of duty required.

We are not party to the exchange of emotions between them.

TWO

The North West Passage

The notion that there existed a sea passage across the north of America, linking the Atlantic Ocean to the Pacific, has a very long history. The 'South West Passage' through the Straits of Magellan had been discovered in 1520. It had always been assumed that the American landmass did not extend as far as the North Pole and that there was therefore a North West Passage waiting to be discovered.

As early as 1497, when John Cabot sailed in the *Matthew* from Bristol, he reached the Newfoundland Banks and he hoped a further search would find a route across the Atlantic to Cathay. The Elizabethan explorers began the search in earnest in 1578 when Martin Frobisher sailed northwards along the coast of Greenland. He discovered what was erroneously called the Frobisher Straits off Baffin Island. He was convinced that there was a passage to the west, but his straits turned out to be no more than a very deep bay. The Labrador current, flowing to the south, seemed to imply that there was a great ocean somewhere beyond to the north and west. In the 1580s the explorer John Davis penetrated well inside the Arctic Circle to a latitude of more than 72° in what became known as Baffin Bay. He was forced back again by the contrary winds and the lateness of the season but he noted that there was a tidal flow from the Hudson Straits and this suggested that the passage they sought might be in that location.

In 1607 Henry Hudson sailed through the straits named after him and he entered the vast waters and the ice floes of Hudson Bay. There were many islands and inlets and it would take years to explore them all. The false belief developed that one of the inlets into Hudson Bay was the entrance to the North West Passage, a belief which continued until the nineteenth century. Hudson's voyage was followed by another remarkable voyage in 1610 when William Baffin penetrated as far north as 76° into the northern latitudes of Baffin Bay. Baffin sailed to the west through Lancaster Sound. If he could have held his course for another 800 miles he would have entered the Beaufort Sea and he might have discovered the passage — but his wooden ship and all his crew would have perished in the attempt. Instead he headed south again into Hudson Bay and he was forced to return home before his ship became trapped in the ice.

The next serious attempt to discover the passage was made in 1631 when two rival expeditions set out from London and Bristol. The London expedition was captained by Luke Foxe who had something in common with James Cook in that he was a Yorkshireman. The Bristol expedition was captained by Thomas James. At one point the two ships actually met up with each other on the bleak coast of Hudson Bay. The two captains were polite and they dined and entertained each other in their cabins. They did not join forces. Foxe explored to the north of Hudson Bay and returned to England before the winter set in. James decided to winter on Hudson Bay, his ship became trapped in the ice and conditions were so bitter than four of his men died, they could not find fresh food and all his men suffered from scurvy. The place where he wintered became known as James Bay. The crew were greatly relieved in the spring when the thaw came and the ship was freed from the ice. The ship spent one more summer exploring Hudson Bay but the expedition found no sign of a passage to the west.

The search was based on two optimistic assumptions. The first was that the passage existed and in this the geographers were correct. The second was the belief that the sea could not freeze over and this assumption was wrong. It was well known that pure water could be obtained from the icebergs and this generated a theory that the icebergs were created in freshwater rivers, which carried them to the sea. It was incorrectly reasoned that the North West Passage could not freeze over. What they did not know was that it needed a massive powered iron ship and an icebreaker to batter a way through the ice.

The Hudson Bay Company was created in the seventeenth century to trade in furs and minerals. As a result of the trade the coastline of the bay became better known and in 1719 an expedition was sent from the company's trading post at Churchill to the north of Hudson Bay under the command of James Knight. Nothing more was heard of Knight's ill fated expedition until nearly fifty years later when the macabre wreckage of his ships was found in five fathoms of water off Marble Island. A house and humble graves were found, it was obvious that all the expedition had perished in the bitter winter. This did not deter the Hudson Bay Company from making another search and in 1741 when Christopher Middleton made another voyage to the northern end of Hudson Bay, he was sponsored by the Irish Member of Parliament, Arthur Dobbs. Middleton wintered at Fort Churchill by consent of the Hudson Bay Company. He claimed to have found a flood tide entering the bay from the west but he could find no sign of a passage from whence it came. When Middleton returned home his sponsor Arthur Dobbs accused him of negligence and corruption, he claimed that the Hudson Bay Company were jealous of their franchise in the fur trade and that they did not want to encourage traffic through Hudson Bay. The next attempt to find the passage was in 1766 when Samuel Hearne made a voyage from Fort Churchill to the north. Hearne returned the following year, claiming to have sailed to a latitude of over 71° north. He found nothing of note and he came home convinced that there was no such thing as a North West Passage through Hudson Bay.

One more British expedition to the Atlantic end must be mentioned. It was sponsored in 1773 by the Royal Society when two ships called the *Racehorse* and *Carcass* were specially strengthened to help them to navigate through the ice. These ships returned from

Baffin Bay with nothing of great value but the expedition is of interest on two counts. Firstly it was the first expedition to get within 10° of the North Pole and secondly one of the crew members was an unknown boy of sixteen called Horatio Nelson, a reminder that the naval careers of Cook and Nelson overlapped by about six years.

It all seemed a very extravagant waste of time and money. But the existence of a passage would save a great deal of time and money for the merchants trading with the east. The belief in the existence of the North West Passage continued and the British government offered a prize of twenty thousand pounds to anybody who could find the passage. This was exactly the same as the sum offered to any person who could solve the problem of finding the longitude at sea. Other nations had tried to find the passage but they met with no more success. All the expeditions, British, French and Spanish had been failures. The evidence in favour of a passage was very slender and unreliable. But surely, thought the British admiralty, if the passage did exist then it would be possible to find it from the Pacific. With this approach a ship sailing the cold waters to the north of America would be safer with the knowledge that it would sooner or later enter known seas and could make for the trading posts on Hudson Bay.

Interest moved to consider the Pacific entrance to the North West Passage and in 1761 the German cartographer, Gerhard Muller published a book called *Voyages from Asia to America* which was a valuable collection of maps and included the latest Russian discoveries in the Bering Sea. Only isolated landfalls were plotted on the American coast with broken lines as conjecture in between. It did show the existence of the Bering Strait between Asia and America but Muller had found no detail of a sea passage to the north of America. There was another map included in Muller's book, showing the alleged discoveries of Juan de Fuca and Admiral de Fonte in the sixteenth and seventeenth centuries. He published a wonderful map with a great West Sea, discovered by Fuca in 1592, covering the whole of the Arizona desert. At about the 55th parallel a series of lakes and channels connected all the way through Canada to reach the northern coast of Hudson Bay and a second deep channel to the north reached almost to Baffin Bay with a narrow isthmus between Pacific and Atlantic waters. It was a wonderful conjecture but it was all fiction, it was based on a far too literal interpretation of crude sketches from a voyage made many generations before.

In 1774 however, a much more detailed map was published by the Russians in a book by the Russian geographer Stahlin called *An Account of the New Northern Archipelago*. The Aleutian Archipelago and the Bering Strait were clearly shown on the map and there was also a fictitious channel cutting right through Alaska showing the obvious route to the north of America. The publication caused quite a stir in the shipping world, the British had never explored so far north in the Pacific Ocean and they had no reason to suspect the accuracy of Stahlin's carefully drawn map.

Recent progress in exploration meant that ships could be provisioned for longer voyages. The risk of scurvy was not fully eliminated but it was much less of a problem than it had been twenty years earlier. The art of navigation had made major steps forward. Thanks to John Harrison's work on the ship's chronometer any ship carrying such an instrument could calculate its position very accurately anywhere on the earth's surface. The method of lunars had also been perfected by the astronomers at the Royal Greenwich Observatory and, even though the method did not give as simple or as accurate a longitude as the chronometer, it provided a valuable check on the errors of the watch. These developments meant that it was perfectly possible to send an expedition all the way round to the northern Pacific to search for the North West Passage from the western end.

There were other objects to the voyage. Cook wanted to return Omai to his own people. He also wanted to rediscover and locate the island discovered by Kerguelen in the Indian Ocean. He wanted to sail the north west coast of America and to make maps and charts of the coastline. To get his ships into the Pacific Cook decided it was better to sail eastward via the Cape of Good Hope than to sail westward around Cape Horn. The time difference was in favour of the Cape

Horn route but on his first voyage Cook still remembered the problems he had had trying to reprovision the ship at Rio de Janeiro. Cape
Town was a far better provisioned place than Rio, it was on the main
trade route to the Orient, it was an excellent place to purchase supplies
and to service the ships for a long voyage. This was the decisive factor
in the choice between the two routes.

The time had come to choose the ships and to muster the crews.
The *Resolution* was under overhaul and refitting at the Deptford yard
after her three year voyage. She would soon be available for another
voyage. No ship had performed better than the *Resolution* for Cook's
purposes and there was therefore no question that she would sail on his
third voyage. The *Adventure* had performed far less well and in any case
she was not available, but Cook had no difficulty in finding a replacement in the shape of the *Diligence*, a vessel of 298 tons and only
eighteen months old. It comes as no surprise to find that she was a
North Sea collier built in Langbourne's yard at Whitby on similar lines
to his other ships. She was purchased for £1,865 and was renamed the
Discovery. She was smaller than the *Resolution* and she carried only two
masts but a further £550 was spent on restructuring and work was put
in hand to upgrade her to a three master. She was filled and sheathed
against the teredo worm. She was fitted with eight four-pounder
cannon, eight swivel guns and eight musquetoons. The *Resolution*
carried twelve swivel guns and twelve musquetoons, the numbers are
roughly in proportion to the size and complement of the two ships.

There were plenty of men willing to sign on for another voyage
with Captain Cook. He was well known to be a humane captain. He
took great care of his ship, he took the greatest precautions to keep his
men healthy and he went to great pains to provide the best diet of
fresh food available within the restrictions of a long voyage. The
American War of Independence was a factor which told in Cook's
favour. Things were going very badly in America and many would be
called to fight against their cousins in the very unpopular revolution
across the Atlantic. Some thought it better to sign up for a voyage of
discovery than to fight against the Americans. It must also be said

however, that there were plenty of men who were not prepared to sign up for another voyage with Captain Cook, the reason being that they were signing away three or four years of their lives. Cook's voyages were far longer than any others in the British navy.

Cook's first lieutenant was John Gore aged forty-six, a veteran of the *Endeavour* voyage and one of the few survivors from the *Dolphin* voyage who could claim to have circumnavigated the globe before Cook. Gore had missed out on Cook's second voyage only because of his commitments to Joseph Banks. Cook's second lieutenant was the very competent James King, a well-educated young man from the inland town of Clitheroe in Lancashire, where his father had been the curate of Clitheroe parish church. King had studied science at both Paris and Oxford and he knew his astronomy well enough to help with the navigation.

Of those who were eager to sign up none was more enthusiastic than James Burney, and it happens that his life is more closely documented than the majority of Cook's crew. At the time Cook was mustering his crew Burney was already serving his country in America. He was on the *Cerberus* patrolling the American seaboard. His sister Fanny wrote to her correspondent Samuel Crisp with a few details, she was fully aware that James would want to volunteer for Cook's voyage:

> You enquire so much after Jem [James] that I am tempted to send You one of his Letters to me, in which he gives a good & satisfactory account of his Captain & fellow Lieutenant. He Corresponds with me with tolerable regularity; where he at present is I am not certain, but I fancy still at Portsmouth. It is true that there have been Removals among the officers of this ship, in so much that only the 1st Lieutenant remains the same as when Jem went on Board. The Cerberus is ordered to carry the three General officers, viz General Burgoigne, Gen Cleveland & another, to America, but we have no certain information at present when they will sail. Jem in his Last Letter tells me that he is quite in the Dark about it himself. There is much talk of [an

in]tended South Sea Expedition; Now You must [know] there is
nothing that Jem so earnestly desires as to be of the Party, & my
Father has made great Interest at the Admiralty to procure him that
pleasure: & as it is not to be undertaken till Capt. Cooke's return, it
is just possible that Jem may be returned in Time from America.[1]

James did in fact manage to get back from America in time to sign on
for the voyage, and he was delighted to be appointed first lieutenant of
the *Discovery*. He was not the only man from Cook's second voyage to
sign on for the third voyage. There was William Anderson, the Scottish
surgeon who kept an excellent journal and William Ellis the surgeon's
mate. There was the Cornishman William Lanyon who had served on
the *Adventure*. There was George Vancouver who claimed to have sailed
further south than any man alive. It was he who scampered out along
the jib sail and waved his hat at the sailors when the icicles covered the
ship in the bitter cold of the Antarctic seas and the *Resolution* reached
a latitude of over 70° south. In all there were more than twenty men
who had sailed in various capacities on Cook's second voyage. We
should also mention at this point the eighteen-year-old George
Gilbert, a midshipman on the *Resolution*; he had not sailed with Cook
before but he was the son of Joseph Gilbert, master of the same ship
on Cook's second voyage.

The captain of the *Discovery*, and therefore second in command of
the expedition, was Charles Clerke aged thirty-five, another veteran of
the *Endeavour* and also a veteran of Cook's second voyage on the
Resolution.

Charles Clerke was one of a select few who sailed on all three of
Cook's voyages of exploration, he was third lieutenant on board the
Endeavour and second lieutenant of the *Resolution* on the second voyage.
Clerke's first lieutenant was James Burney, and the relatively unknown
John Rickman was his second lieutenant. William Peckover, a gunner,
had been a gunner's mate on the *Resolution* and an able bodied seaman
on the *Endeavour*. Robert Anderson from Inverness, another gunner, had
been quartermaster on the *Endeavour*. William Harvey, a Londoner and

the master's mate had been a midshipman on both of Cook's previous voyages. William Collett from High Wycombe was master at arms on the second voyage and an able bodied seaman on the *Endeavour*. John Ramsey from Perthshire was a cook on the *Resolution* and he had also sailed on the *Endeavour*. There was also Samuel Gibson, sergeant of the marines and a veteran of the south seas at the age of twenty-seven. Gibson is an especially interesting case. He narrowly escaped a flogging from Cook on the *Endeavour* voyage when he tried to desert with a Tahitian girl, yet he remained loyal to Cook for all three voyages and went around the ship boasting that he had saved the captain's life in a skirmish with the Maoris.

There were of course many who were sailing for the first time with Cook. His second lieutenant, James King, was one who has already been mentioned. King's great friend was also called James, he was James Trevenen who, as his name implies, was from a Cornish family. Trevenen was a highly sensitive and literate man and his account of the voyage included a few rare personal details of the personnel involved, including a unique description of one occasion when Captain Cook dropped his guard and shared a joke with the junior officers. In later life Trevenen used to take off his coat to display his tattoos to the ladies, and we may assume that the tattoos were souvenirs of Polynesia and that he dined out on his memoirs of Captain Cook.

The ship's master was one William Bligh, at this time a young man of twenty-two, but destined to become the governor of New South Wales. He is remembered by posterity for the infamous mutiny on the *Bounty*. He was an excellent and steady seaman but with an impetuous and violent temper which created very great human problems in later life; these problems began to surface with Cook late in the voyage when Bligh began to see James King as an imposter. Edward Riou from Faversham in Kent should be mentioned in the same breath as Bligh for both men came to serve under Nelson. In April 1801, at the battle of Copenhagen, Bligh was captain of the 56-gun *Glatton* and Riou commanded the 38-gun *Amazon*. It was at Copenhagen, much to Nelson's grief, that Riou lost his life. It is a sobering thought that

Horatio Nelson himself could have signed up for Cook's third voyage. The hero of Trafalgar was an unknown seventeen-year-old midshipman when the crews were being mustered but, as we have seen, even at this tender age he had sailed inside the Arctic Circle. In 1776 Nelson had just returned from Bombay on the *Dolphin*. He was taken very ill with a fever and for this reason he was unable to sign up for another voyage until after Cook's ships had sailed.

The third lieutenant in the *Resolution* was John Williamson, of Irish descent. He was an honest and obedient man but he had a communication problem and, as subsequent events showed, he was not the ideal man for an expedition of this nature. He had a commendable naval career and he rose to become a captain but his career ended when he was court-martialled for 'unsatisfactory behaviour' after the battle of Camperdown in 1797.

The *Resolution* carried a complement of twenty marines and the *Discovery* carried fifteen. Their officer was Lieutenant Molesworth Phillips who was recommended for the voyage by Joseph Banks. Molesworth Phillips made another Burney family connection, he was a great friend of James Burney and after the voyage married Susan Burney, the sister of James and Fanny. John Ledyard, a corporal of the marines, is an interesting case in that he was born in America but he refused to fight for American independence and signed up instead for the British. When he returned from the voyage he was asked to fight on the British side against the Americans. He refused to take sides again though it probably cost him his commission.

The ship's surgeons were William Anderson, a Scottish veteran of the second voyage, his mate was the Welshman David Samwell. Both these men kept interesting and valuable journals. Samwell was the son of a parson but this did not inhibit his admiration of the opposite sex and he frequently commented on the beauty of the Polynesian girls. William Ellis was the surgeon's mate on the *Discovery*, he was Cambridge educated and he was patronised by Joseph Banks. He was an amateur draughtsman and he sometimes painted in water colours. Joseph Banks had no intention of going on the voyage, but we have already seen his influence in choosing the crew. Relations between Joseph Banks and James Cook remained excellent and the episode of the previous voyage, when Banks made an unsuccessful move to take over the command of the expedition, was buried and forgotten.

The supernumeries were not as many as on the previous voyages. There was, of course, Omai, a passenger to Tahiti. There was the talented artist John Webber who joined the expedition at Plymouth. He was primarily a landscape artist, the son of a Swiss sculptor and educated at Berne and Paris, but he had a marvellous eye for detail and his portraits were also of great value. Cook's lieutenant, James King made the correct but unfortunate observation that the ship was not as well supplied with scientists as the previous two voyages. His remark prompted an explosion from Captain Cook who had had a bellyful of scientists after his relations with Johann Rienhold Forster on his second voyage. The captain pronounced good riddance to all philosophers and cursed them with a seaman's oath. The botanical and zoological factions took on a lower profile than on the previous voyages, but Joseph Banks did send along David Nelson, a botanist from Kew gardens. Nelson sailed on the smaller vessel, the *Discovery*. We cannot pass him by without a mention of his subsequent career for David Nelson also sailed with Bligh on the *Bounty* to supervise the collection of the breadfruit at Tahiti. He was set adrift with Bligh after the mutiny and he died in Timor of fever and exposure.

The expedition's astronomer was William Bayly, also sailing on the *Discovery*, he was well known to Cook for he had sailed on Cook's second voyage with Tobias Furneaux on the *Adventure*. The *Resolution* did not carry an official astronomer, this was because of the success of the chronometer for finding the longitude, but both Cook and King were very capable astronomical observers and only one official astronomer was therefore deemed to be necessary.

By June the provisioning was almost complete, the ships were refurbished and ready to go to sea. There was a touch of drama with the *Discovery* for Captain Charles Clerke was unable to take the helm. Clerke was a good-natured man, and he had foolishly stood surety for the debts of his brother Sir John Clerke. For this he had been thrown into the debtor's prison. The expedition could not wait for the wheels of justice to turn and the *Discovery* sailed for Plymouth without her captain. This was to the great joy of the Burney family who had difficulty curbing their desire to rush en masse to the south coast so that they could witness their darling James, the first lieutenant, commanding the ship on her passage down the English Channel. Fanny wrote to her correspondent Samuel Crisp:

> But the Great man of men is your friend James — who is now, in Fact, & in power, Captain of his ship, though, alas — not in Honour or Profit. The Case is, Captain Clarke has obtained permission to stay some Time longer in Town, to settle his affairs, &, in the hope of profiting by some Act — that I don't very well understand, concerning Debtors, he has surrendered himself, & is now actually in the King's bench. An order had been sent from the Admiralty, To our Lieutenant, to carry the ship himself to Plymouth. And further of his affairs, I know not myself, nor whether he is yet sailed, not anything about him. We have never seen his sweet Face since the last that I saw yours & that glorious Confusion to which you was a Witness, was, I presume, meant by way of tender Farwell of the House. He was stopt in the Portland Road, by contrary Winds, & took that opportunity of writing to my Father...[2]

Cook's journal of the voyage opens on 10 February when he was given his commission, but he made only three small entries before June. On 10 June he took on board a bull with two cows and their calves with 'a great quantity of Hay and Corne for thier subsistance', this was not fresh meat for the voyage, his plan was to present the animals to the Tahitians to stock their islands. A few more crew were mustered to replace the fifty or so who had deserted. The scientific and navigational equipment was taken on board. The chronometer by Kendall, which earned such high praise from Cook, was 3 minutes and 31 seconds slow by Greenwich time. It was serviced and calibrated in preparation for the long journey ahead.

There was a dinner on board the *Resolution* at Long Reach with Lord Sandwich and Hugh Palliser, the top brass from the admiralty. They were saluted with seventeen guns. Then the *Resolution* left the Thames for Plymouth. Cook himself said his farewells on 24 June when he left home at six in the morning. He characteristically gives no details of this moving event, his parting from his wife and family consisting of Elizabeth, James and Nathaniel plus the new baby, a tiny red-faced child christened Hugh, whom he held in his arms for the last time. He travelled to Chatham with Omai and he arrived at Plymouth on the last day of the month. From there he wrote to Lord Sandwich:

> I cannot leave England without taken some method to thank your Lordship for the many favors confered upon me, and in particular for the Very liberal allowance made to Mrs Cook during my absence. This, by enabling my family to live at ease and removing from them every fear of indigency has set my heart at rest and filled it with gratitude to my Noble benefactor. If a faithfull discharge of that duty which your Lordship has intrusted to my care, be any return, it shall be my first and principal object.
>
> I was to have spoke to your Lordship in behalf of Mrs Mahone, Widow of the late Cook of the Adventure, who is minuted down for a Nurse to Greenwich Hospital, a place she seems very suitable for, if your Lor[d]ship should have an opportunity to appoint her it will add to the many favors already centered on
>
> My Lord
Your Lordships Most faithfull and Most
Obedient Humble Servant
James Cook[3]

The cook mentioned in the second paragraph is not a relative, but the ship's cook Mortimer Mahony who sailed on the *Adventure*. James Cook had no respect at all for him because he was dirty and lazy and, by ignoring Cook's orders, he was probably the person directly responsible for the only serious outbreak of scurvy on any of Cook's voyages. James Cook was still prepared to put in a word for his widow.

On 4 July 1776 the ships were both in Plymouth harbour. On that day, on the other side of the Atlantic Ocean, the American Congress in Philadelphia signed the Declaration of Independence. Cook's ship sailed before the news of the declaration reached England, but he chose to leave Plymouth without his consort, the *Discovery*. Captain Clerke was expected at Plymouth within a few days but nobody knew for sure how long it would take him to extricate himself from his financial problems.

At last the great voyage was under way. The ship was straining at the seams, loaded with cattle and livestock, a full complement of men, scientific instruments, maps and charts. The *Resolution* beat her way again out of Plymouth Sound on her way to the far ends of the earth, she passed Smeaton's masterpiece, the Eddystone lighthouse completed in 1759. It was an emotional departure but for many of the experienced sailors it had happened several times before. They knew well enough the dangers of the voyage and they confidently expected another triumphant return in three or four years' time. The wind swelled the sails, the masts bent and the ship leaned to starboard. The onlookers on Plymouth Hoe saw the beautiful sight of a three master in full sail headed for the other side of the world to journey through seas where no ship had sailed before, powered only by wind and current and forces of nature.

THREE

England to Cape Town

Cook decided to make his first port of call at Tenerife. The *Resolution* anchored in the road at Santa Cruz to take on fresh water and food supplies. At Santa Cruz he met a French captain named Borda and a Spanish surveyor called Varila. The captains had something in common, for the French and Spanish were testing a chronometer with which they were attempting to fix the longitude of the Peak of Tenerife. It was part of a project to improve the charts of the area. Cook knew how reliable Kendall's chronometer had been on his previous voyage and he estimated the longitude to be 17° 00' 30". It happened that by pure coincidence there was a total eclipse of the moon on the very night they were there. Cook observed part of the eclipse but he was frustrated by cloud cover. He was able to estimate a longitude of 16° 30' 21" from his astronomical data, a discrepancy of about 20 nautical miles. The Spaniard Varila very rightly did not claim to know the longitude to within seconds of arc and he calculated 16° 46', a figure very close to the mean of Cook's two estimates. The true longitude is now accepted as 16° 38' West which shows that even with the best instruments of the times it was impossible to estimate the longitude to better than 10 nautical miles in the eighteenth century.

Cook bought a good supply of hay and corn to feed all his livestock. He filled the water casks and smoked the ship for reasons of hygiene.

The *Resolution* stayed three days at Tenerife, then Cook sailed for Porta Praya in the Cape Verde Islands optimistically hoping to find that the *Discovery* had got there before him. He had no idea at all of how far the second ship was behind him, but when he arrived there was no sign of his consort so he did not put into port. Another problem had surfaced already, a problem destined to plague him for the whole voyage. The *Resolution* was not the ship he had known of old and she was leaking badly at the seams. He recorded the problems in his log:

... the weather was generally dark and gloomy, with frequent rains of which we saved as much Water as filled the most of our empty water casks. These rains and the close sultry weather they accompany but too often bring on sickness in this passage, one has at least every thing to fear from them, and cannot be too much on ones guard, by obliging the people to dry their cloathes and airing the Ship with fires and smoke at every oppertunity. This was constantly practised on board the *Resolution* & *Discovery* and we certainly profited by it, for we had fewer sick than on either of my former Voyages. We had however the Mortification to find the Ship exceeding leaky in all her upper works, the hot and dry weather we had just past through had opened her Seams, which had been badly Caulked at first, so wide that they admited the rain Water through as it fell and there was hardly a Man that could lie dry in his bed; the officers in the gunroom were all driven out of their cabbins by the Water that came thro' the sides. The sails in the Sail rooms got wet and before we had weather to dry them, many of them were quite ruined and occasioned a great expence of Canvas & time to make them in some degree serviceable. This complaint of our sail rooms we experienced on my late Voyage and was represented to the yard officers who undertook to remove it, but it did not appear to me that any thing had been done that could answer that end. To repair these defects the Caulkers were set to work as soon as we got into fair settled Weather, to caulk the Decks and inside Weather works of the Ship, for I would not trust them over the side while at sea. [1]

There was little they could do before reaching Cape Town, but at least they were in the tropics and the water was not the freezing Arctic seas they would have to experience later in the voyage. They had been holding a southerly course for about five days when the surgeon William Anderson spotted breaking water ahead of the ship. Anderson was not a sailor but he knew the breakers spelt danger, probably from hidden rocks just beneath the water. He was wondering whether or not to raise the alarm when Captain Cook appeared beside him. The captain immediately yelled an order to move hard to starboard and as the ship turned a whole range of breakers became visible with the ship bearing down rapidly upon them. It was obvious that the ship was heading for a reef of hidden rocks just below the surface. For a period of about ten minutes it looked as though it was impossible to avoid striking the rocks and the expedition was heading for a rapid premature end. The ship changed tack, running parallel to the breakers, and for a time it looked as though she should sail clear. Then the wind changed and the danger was upon them again. The ship seemed to be heading away from the rocks but the swell of the sea was carrying her closer and closer. The *Resolution* just managed to clear the hidden reef, but the danger was not over, another set of breakers appeared ahead, but this time it was only a single rock and the ship was able to avoid it.

Cook characteristically made little of the incident, the rocks were well known and they appeared on all the charts. The responsibility lay with the master William Bligh but Cook carried the ultimate responsibility for his own ship. Anderson was very alarmed, he felt that somebody should be held responsible for such a narrow escape and poor seamanship so soon after leaving England. He concluded that the seamen thought they knew the area well and for that reason they kept a poor watch and they were not taking the necessary precautions. He went on at great length in his journal about the negligence of the crew and the fact that having cleared the danger they simply chose to forget all about it:

To bring a ship into so alarming a situation as we were in at this time without being able to give a satisfactory reason for it certainly deserves the severest reprehension. Humanity will urge innumerable and invincible arguments against the conduct of a person who would risque the destruction of one [person] and certainly much more of above a hundred. Prudence too would remonstrate in such a case and accuse the aggressor of rashness...

This being the case it was not to be suppos'd we were so nigh the land though the event show'd our mistake. But after making the land why not keep clear by standing off till day light or at least some hours. On the contrary in little more than an hour we steerd s[outh] & the consequence was our falling in with these breakers...

It is likewise by no means evident that our situation (I mean the Ships place) was very well known; for in the Evening on asking several people if they expected to see land I was answer'd in such a manner as if they either did not know or car'd little if they did: but it was plain that its appearance was unexpected at the time we saw it as every one was surpriz'd. There likewise appeared a mixture of negligence on this occasion, for it is evident no person was looking out forward or the breakers could not have been discovered first from the quarter, was there any sounding line at hand or anchor unstow'd? Did anybody know what part of the island we were off, how far these rocks extended, or if there was soundings hereabouts? Are these the happy effects of consummate knowledge on Navigation?[2]

The incident was over and forgotten but they were approaching the equator and on 1 September Anderson had something else to complain about:

The afternoon was spent in the old ridiculous ceremony of ducking those who had not cross'd the equator before. This is one of those absurd customs which craft and inconsiderate levity has imposed on mankind and which every sensible person who has it in his power ought to suppress instead of encouraging.[3]

The sailors took no notice of the opinions of a mere surgeon. They were not to be denied their horseplay and thirty-five newcomers to the southern hemisphere were ducked. For Captain Cook, who had crossed the equator five times in the Atlantic, it was all a repeat performance and he did not even record it in his journal. He was more interested in the steady wind from the south east which took him further west than he might have chosen but he knew that if he continued to sail to the south the winds would become more westerly. He came within 30 leagues of the coast of Brazil before swinging to the east and setting a course for the Cape of Good Hope. On 7 August Anderson looked for the coast of Brazil but it was too far away and he saw nothing. This was an uneventful part of the voyage, but when September arrived the ship was quite close to the African coast and the number of birds following the ship was on the increase. They began to alight on the rigging and scavenge for food. An albatross followed the ship. There were flights of pintadoes, three penguins were sighted, an antarctic fulmar, and Port Egmont hen. A flight of blue petrels appeared and a large brown petrel with a white bill. A noddy settled on the rigging, it was a black bird with webbed feet and a white head and it paid the price by being caught and eaten. Flying fish appeared alongside and accompanied the ship on part of its journey. In October there was a luminous glow of the sea at night, caused by a large population of opal salps which were a common sight in the seas near the cape.

The Cape of Good Hope was sighted on 17 October and the next day the *Resolution* was anchored safely in Table Bay. The first leg of the voyage was over and the passage from Plymouth had taken ninety-eight days. There was much to do after so long at sea. The bull and the cows were set to pasture, a welcome relief for them after so long on deck, and the sheep were taken ashore and put in a pen. Cook was able to do some recaulking on the ship to try and plug the leaks but he was angered by the bad workmanship of the Deptford Yard when the ship-wrights had had many months to make the ship seaworthy and he was concerned about what other scrimped labour he might find. Whilst they were at Cape Town they witnessed a shipwreck, a homeward bound ship had broken her anchor cable and had been driven on shore by heavy seas. The crew were saved but the local inhabitants, like coastal populations the world over, had scavenged the wreck and taken everything of value.

Cook ordered fresh bread to be baked. The bakers were willing enough to supply the *Resolution* but when he ordered the same for the *Discovery* they dragged their heels, they did not wish to commit themselves until they saw the ship arrive. Cook's crew had to wait an unknown length of time for the *Discovery* and this left them plenty of time for socialising. Cook had been at Cape Town three times before, once on the return from his *Endeavour* voyage and twice on his second voyage with the *Resolution*. Cape Town was the essential port of call on the route to the Orient, it was a seafaring town with a great interest in shipping, commerce and exploration. The Dutch were very knowledgeable about Cook's previous voyages and he was treated as a celebrity. Joachim van Plettenburg had been promoted from acting governor to governor since the last time Cook had met him. He entertained Cook and his officers at the governor's residence and Captain Cook was promised every assistance he needed. Cook's own thoughts were rather more cynical, he thought that the dealers had a monopoly and that all the goods and services were overpriced. 'In short the Dutch in this affair strictly adhered to the maxim they have laid down at this place which is to get as much by strangers as they possibly can without ever considering [whether] the means are justifiable or not.'

The crew enjoyed the social life and David Samwell, the surgeon's mate, wrote to his friend Matthew Gregson in Liverpool. It was a very optimistic letter suggesting that he could be back in England by the following winter after discovering the North West Passage:

We arrived here all hearty the 19th inst after a pleasant Passage of something better than three months. We called in our way and staid 3 Days at the Island of Teneriffe taking in Wine and other Refreshments — the Cape is a very plentiful Country & we live upon the Fat of the

Land during our stay which will be about a Month, then we shall set off for Otaheite where we expect to be about the time you will receive this Letter which I imagine will be some time in Febry or March. I do not suppose we shall stay long at Otaheite as we must embrace the summer season to try for the North west passage; if we find it we shall be in England next Winter. We have various Opinions about it some think we shall & others that we shall not find it.[4]

Samwell had taken an interest in Omai during the Atlantic passage and his comments were much in keeping with those of the Burneys. We find that Omai had learnt to play cards, although his friend James Burney was on the other ship it was probably Jem who had taught the Tahitian to play:

Omiah is very hearty and I do not doubt but he will live to see his own Country again, he is not such a stupid fellow as he is generally look'd upon in England, 'tis true he learn'd nothing there but how to play at cards at which he is very expert but I take it to be owing more to his want of Instruction than his want of Capacity to take it. He talks English so bad that a person who does not understand something of his language can hardly understand him or make himself understood by him they have made him more of the fine Gentleman than anything else. He is a good natur'd fellow enough, and like all ignorant People very superstitious, Seeing on our Passage here a very bright Meteor pointing to the Northward, he said it was God going to England & was very Angry that any one should offer to contradict him, looking upon it as no less than Blasphemy. Whether there is any strange God come amongst You is more than I can say, as I have not faith enough to believe that Omiah is a Seer.[5]

In his last paragraph Samwell describes Cape Town and the pleasures thereof. He found the place far more amenable than Santa Cruz in Tenerife. He comments on the love of pleasure and on the respect which the residents showed towards Captain Cook:

I live on shore in a Tent close to the Town which is called Cape Town
& is beyond exception the most beautiful I ever saw — amongst the
Spaniards at Santa Cruz there was nothing to be seen but a pack of
lazy damn'd Priests, but here we have people who cultivate their Lands
build handsome Towns & are much given to Dancing & merriment,
and if such people as these are not more agreeable in the Eyes both of
God & Man than a sett of gloomy, bigotted, praying Priest ridden
Miscreants then I'll be damned.

Today Capt. Cook din'd with the Governor at the Garrison — 3 royal
Salutes of 21 Guns each were given with the Toasts at Dinner. The
Governor & all at the Cape pay Captn Cook extraordinary Respect, he
is as famous here & more noted perhaps than in England.[6]

Anderson's journal confirms the hospitality of the residents. He
visited Stellenbosch, a settlement about twenty miles east of Cape
Town. There he found about thirty houses with cornfields and vineyards. He and his party were received at the house of a Mr Cloeder
where they were not only wined and dined but treated to musical
accompaniment as well:

Little wind with fine clear weather. In the morning we left Stellenboch
and soon arriv'd at the house we pass'd on Saturday whose owner [Mr
Cloeder] had sent us an invitation the evening before to visit him.
This Gentleman entertain'd us with the greatest hospitality and in a
manner very different from what we expected. He receiv'd us with
music and a band also play'd while we din'd, which considering the
situation of the place might be reckon'd elegant. He show'd us his
Wine cellars, his Orchards and Vineyards, all which I must own
inspir'd me with a wish to know in what manner these industrious
people could raise such plenty in a spot where I believe no other
European nation would have attempted to settle. In the afternoon we
cross'd the country and pass'd a few plantations, one of which seem'd

very considerable, and laid out in a taste somewhat different from any other we saw. In the evening we arriv'd at a farm house which is the first in the cultivated tract call'd the Pearl, and we had at the same time a view of Drakenstein, the third Colony of this country, which lyes along by the foot of the lofty hills already mentioned and contains several farms or plantations which are not very extensive.[7]

On 10 November came the news they had all been waiting for when the topsails of the *Discovery* appeared on the horizon. The celebrations were a little premature. The ship was sailing smoothly into the harbour between Penguin Island and the Sugar Loaf when a light offshore breeze caught the sails. Suddenly the ship was found to be driving rapidly onto Penguin Island with darkness falling fast. A bower anchor was cast but it failed to find a grip on the bottom and the wind suddenly came on in very strong gusts from the hills, driving the *Discovery* towards the rocks around the island. Every person aboard expected the ship to be thrown onto the rocks but luckily the anchor found something to grapple and held them steady. At ten o'clock they started to take the anchor in but before they could get it out of the water a tidal current swung the ship around creating great confusion. It was midnight before they had the anchor out of the water. Luckily the wind had dropped, they were able to sail into the passage between the islands and to anchor there safely until the morning.

To have a consort made all the difference to morale and the next day, after the night of drama, the men of the *Resolution* gave the *Discovery* three rousing cheers. The smaller ship claimed to have been delayed by a week by bad weather which blew them back to sea after sighting the African coast, but she had still made a good passage from Plymouth in 102 days. They had one fatality when George Harrison, corporal of marines, was lost at sea but it was a happy reunion and there were great celebrations by both of the ships' companies. The *Discovery* carried a letter from Joseph Banks to James Cook. The captain replied to his old shipmate, including a little gossip about Omai whom we find had enjoyed a cabin large enough to stable four horses. The Polynesian was obliged to surrender his cabin as the *Resolution* came to bear even more resemblance to Noah's Ark:

> Your very obliging favour I received by Captain Clerke who arrived here on the 18th Inst. something more than three weeks after me and [in] nearly the same time as I sailed from Plymouth before him, for I left that place on the 13th of July. We are now ready to proceed on our Voyage, and nothing is wanting but a few females of our own species to make the *Resolution* a compleate ark for I have added considerably to the Number of Animals I took onboard in England. Omai consented with raptures to give up his Cabbin to make room for four Horses — He continues to enjoy a good state of health and great flow of spirits, and has never once given me the l[e]ast reason to find fault with any part of his conduct. He desires his best respects to you, Dr Solander, Lord Seaford and to a great many more, Ladies as well as Gentlemen, whose names I cannot insert because they would fill up this sheet of paper, I can only say that he does not forget any who have shewed him the least kindness.
>
> I am greatly obliged to you for your readiness to describe the Plants which are to be published in my Journal and I hope Mr Strahan will give you the parts in time. I have no other way of makeing a return for this and many other favours than by using my best endeavours to add to your Collection of Plants & Animals: this you may be assured of, and that the Man you have sent out with Captain Clerke to collect seeds & plants shall have every assistance in my power to give him...[8]

These sentiments contrast sharply with Cook's outburst against poor James King at the mention of scientists, but no doubt Cook had his ups and downs like other men and he certainly valued the support of men like Joseph Banks. On the last day of November the ship was ready to sail. The expedition was fortunate in that so far there had been no major calamities on the voyage, but both ships had had a narrow escape from the rocks and both vessels were badly in need of re-caulking when they arrived. There was a problem over the sheep at Cape Town, dogs had deliberately been set loose in the pen so that the sheep would escape and could be taken by thieves. It was summer in the southern hemisphere but by the time they got to search for the North West Passage it would be late summer in the northern hemisphere and too late to spend much time in colder climates. The delays had made the expedition late and they were behind schedule. What the men did not know, for Cook was not in the habit of telling his men about his plans, was that he intended to look for other islands on the way to Van Dieman's Land and New Zealand.

FOUR

The Indian Ocean

When Captain Cook had been at Cape Town on the return from his second voyage he had met the Frenchman Julien Crozet from whom he obtained information on the discoveries of several islands in the Indian Ocean. Crozet was not the only Frenchman to discover islands in these seas. Captain Marion du Fresne had made discoveries in the same region as also had Yves Joseph Kerguelen. Cook had collected sufficient data on latitudes and longitudes to make a search for these islands and he intended to find them.

The *Resolution* and *Discovery* weighed anchor on the last day of November but the winds did not oblige and they had to wait for the morning before they could leave Table Bay. On 1 December they rounded the southernmost point of the African continent, the Cape of Good Hope, at a comfortable distance of seven leagues and they entered the Indian Ocean. Cook set a course of WSW, he did not intend to run along the latitude for several reasons. Firstly he knew that something close to a great circle route to New Zealand would be shorter, secondly he wanted to take advantage of the roaring forties but thirdly, and most important, he knew that there existed islands in the Indian Ocean which he had not seen and which were not fully charted.

Now that Cook had the data from his visits to Cape Town he felt confident of finding the islands sighted by Fresne and Crozet and also the land found by Kerguelen in 1772. Only twelve days out from Cape Town he had his first success and Marion Island was sighted. There was a small island to the north which he named Prince Edward Island. He judged Marion Island to be about 15 leagues in circumference and Prince Edward Island about 9. The ships sailed between the islands which were steep and rocky with mountains towering to four thousand feet, but there was no sign of a tree or even a shrub and it would be hard to imagine a more isolated and inhospitable speck of land. Cook measured the positions but he did not attempt a landing. He knew from his conversation with Captain Crozet that there were other islands in the group lying about 12° to the east but they were very small and there was not sufficient time to find them.

It was summer, but the journey was not pleasant for it was still very cold in the high latitudes. The expedition was at least a month behind schedule and unless they could pick up time there could be no Arctic exploration in the next northern summer. The roaring forties lived up to their name, good progress was made but the *Resolution* lost her top mizzen mast in the gales. It was fortunate that the ship carried a replacement and the delay made only a minimal difference to her progress. Four goats and a kid died from exposure on the deck. In spite of the recaulking at Cape Town both ships were leaking and the cold salt water wet the sailors' hammocks which affected their morale. For three more weeks the ships headed to the east and then a thick fog descended. It was impossible to find the position of the ship without a sighting of the sun and the ship's compass was the only guide to the right direction. The ships appeared as ghosts in the fog and much of the time they could not see each other at all. 'In this run', wrote Burney from the *Discovery*, 'we are in continual fear of the two ships parting company, the fogs being so thick and frequently for many hours we have not been able to see twice the length of the ship. Scarce a day passed without losing sight of each other, in these situations we kept company by sound, firing great guns every hour, sometimes oftener and guessing by the report the place of the other ship.' This was exactly the situation in which the *Resolution* and *Adventure* had lost each other four years ago, further south in the same waters, and it was a miracle that the *Resolution* and *Discovery* managed to stay together. But how on earth were they going to find Kerguelen Island when they could hardly see beyond the bowsprit?

Cook pressed on all sail in spite of warnings from Clerke and King that if they did come across Kerguelen Island they could well find themselves wrecked upon it. Here we see James Cook exercising his worst fault. He did not consult his officers in an emergency, he made up his own mind and kept his officers in the dark about his plans. His first lieutenant, James King complained about this lack of communication: 'We who are not acquainted with ye Plan of ye Voyage, nevertheless indulge Conjectures, & conceive that ye smallest delay would hazard ye Loss of a Season, & even the Search for this land, which has already, & may be still Longer detain us, had not been a Part of ye Plan.' But the captain's orders were to sail on through the fog regardless of the danger.

Cook's luck held. It was six in the morning when the fog cleared and land was sighted ahead. The land was a small island offshore from Kerguelen. More islands became visible and by noon the ships were sailing past the mainland. The next day, which happened to be Christmas Day, the *Resolution* anchored in a harbour near a beach of fine dark sand where a few penguins stood in line to receive them. The *Discovery* was some way behind but she anchored at two o'clock in the afternoon. The seamen were delighted to be able to celebrate Christmas Day on *terra firma*.

Kerguelen Island covers an area of about 80 by 60 miles, but the land is so irregular and deeply fjorded that the land area is far less than these dimensions imply. There are no trees and no land birds. Had the island been in the latitude of Tahiti then it would have had a much richer vegetation and it would probably have supported human life, but the latitude was 49° south and it was 3,000 miles from the nearest mainland. The ships arrived in late December, it was midsummer not midwinter, yet the mountain peaks were covered with snow, the land

was cold and inhospitable. Green slopes, which from a distance appeared to be covered by grass, proved to be clothed in no more than moss and lichen. Even the sheep could find nothing to graze on. The one thing Kerguelen had was plenty of fresh water. It might be possible to make a settlement and cultivate crops on the foothills of the mountains, but the island was so desolate and isolated that survival would have been a hard and melancholy existence. Cook made a nominal claim to the island, he knew that the French had a prior claim but it was accepted that any claim to a new land depended on the country being able to make a settlement there and this was something which neither country was prepared to attempt. Anderson's journal records some of the findings, he comments on the French claim and he goes on to describe the landing place with a huge rock towering above it. The artist Webber produced a wash drawing which complements Anderson's description:

> This place lyes exactly in Latd 48 s. Longitude by the dead reckoning 64 :00 East but by the Time keeper 69:11, which is most to be depended on and from our being in it at that time was call'd Christmas harbour. If the French ship who discoverd the land did not anchor here it is plain she had sent in a boat, which to every unprejudic'd person will be a sufficient proof of the right they have to posess it. It may be known by the rock already mentioned from without, and within from a single stone or rock of a vast size which lyes on the top of a hill on the south side near its bottom: there is also one much like it on the north side but a great deal smaller: There is a small beach at its bottom where we commonly landed and behind it some gently rising land on whose top is a large pool of fresh water. The hills are of a moderate height yet many of their tops were cover'd with snow at this time though answering to our June: some of them seem to have suffer'd by earthquakes or other causes, as there are large heaps of stones irregularly heap'd together at their foot or upon their sides. The sides of some which form steep cliffs towards the sea are rent from the top downwards and seem ready to fall off, having stones of a considerable size in these chinks which could not be effected but by a severe shock, unless we suppose they lay just on the top of the place when such an accident (the splitting) happen'd.[1]

He goes on to describe the geology. The soil, if it may warrant the name, seemed to be no more than ground rocks, but it was just capable of supporting some vegetation:

> It may be conceivd notwithstanding this that vegetables may spread; for suppose at the beginning small plants grew only near the shore, they were so rooted as to be able to resist the force of the water and at

the same time stop behind them the small quantity of earth it brought down. The soil increas'd and the plants disseminating would spread gradually up towards the side of the hills and in the most convenient places form a sort of turf, which is the case, and in time perhaps they may reach to the tops of the hills if the climate is not too severe there to permit their growing.

The verdure which appears when at a little distance from the shore would flatter one with the expectation of meeting some herbage, but in this we were much deceiv'd, for that vivid colour was occasion'd only by one very small plant not much unlike some sorts of Saxifrage which grows in large spreading tufts to a considerable height up the sides of the hills. There is indeed one Plant which grows in considerable quantitys on the boggy declivitys to near the height of two feet, somewhat like a small Cabbage when it has shot into seeds. The leaves about the root are numerous, large and rounded with a small point: those on the stalks (which all proceed from the root) are much smaller, oblong and pointed. The stalks, which are often three or four and seperate, run into a cylindrical heads compos'd of small flowers.[2]

Some of the geographical features of the island had already been named by the French, consequently the island acquired a mixture of French and English names. Some of the peninsulas were so long that a close inspection was needed to determine whether they were peninsulas or islands. The French had a solution by using names such as Presqu'île Courbet and Presqu'île Jeanne d'Arc. One of the sailors discovered a bottle hanging from a rock on the north side of the bay. Inside was a Latin inscription which translated into English read 'In the reign of Louis XV, King of France, the lord de Boynes being Secretary of the Marine in the years 1772 and 1773'. Cook knew about Kerguelen's voyage of 1772 but when he left England he knew nothing about the 1773 voyage, also by Kerguelen. He turned the sheet over and on the other side he wrote 'Naves *Resolution* & *Discovery* de Rege Magnae Brittania Decembris 1776'.

Kerguelen Island was a strange, eerie and lifeless world. Cook was pleased to have landed on it but he had no intention of staying longer than necessary. He called it the 'Isle of Desolation'. The stay at Kerguelen lasted only four days, then the ships were back at sea. They ran into thick fog again, they sailed for three hundred leagues without a sight of the sun or the night sky. They were pretty sure that there was no land but they had only the compass with which to check their bearings. Knowing the time at Greenwich was all very well but it was impossible to calculate latitude or longitude without a sight of the sun and an estimate of the local time. There was much concern about the ships losing contact with each other. The days were long and the nights were short but at four o'clock in the morning of 19 January a sudden squall struck the *Resolution* and took away the fore top mast which in turn took the main top gallant mast with it. There was a mess of rigging everywhere and the whole of the next day was lost in trying to clear the tangle of broken wood and rigging from the decks. Was this simply one of the disasters that happened at sea or, like the caulking, was it the fault of the shipwrights in the far away Deptford Yard? James King thought his captain was simply putting on too much sail for the conditions.

Five days later the weather had improved, there was a gentle breeze from the south west accompanied by a great swell from the same quarter. More birds appeared around the ship including several albatrosses, the usual petrels and pintados, some shags, a goodly number of gannets and a flock of unknown birds which Anderson wrongly identified as puffins. When dawn broke there was land just east of north, it was identified as the Mew Stone, the southernmost point of Tasmania, known to Cook as Van Dieman's Land. The land was high, mountain ranges could be seen inland rising one above the other in the distance and although it was midsummer the higher peaks were still covered with snow. There were small rocky islands off the coast, one of the rocks looked so like the Eddystone lighthouse that Cook named it Eddystone rock. There were a few inlets which might have provided an anchorage. The ships sailed to the east and passed a point of land which they identified as Storm Bay where Abel Tasman had anchored many years ago. The wind fell to a very gentle breeze making progress very slow, but at nightfall they identified the cape called Tasman Head at a distance of about four leagues.

Van Dieman's Land was very different from Kerguelen Island. The slopes were thickly forested with trees, the land was inhabited, the smoke from three or four fires could be seen near the shore and when darkness fell the red glow of the flames became visible from the ship. Australians sometimes complain that Cook never returned to their country. They are technically correct but Cook would not have agreed with them for when he landed in Tasmania he was convinced that he had set foot on the southern extremity of New Holland.

There were some on board who had set foot on Tasmania before, they were the men who served on the *Adventure* under Captain Tobias Furneaux on Cook's previous voyage. They included William Anderson the ship's surgeon, Alex Dewar a clerk from Torbay or Dunbar, William Bayly the astronomer, and James Burney who in 1773 was the first Englishman to step onto Tasmanian soil. In 1773 Cook's ships became separated in the southern latitudes and consequently the *Adventure* had made a landfall in Tasmania but the *Resolution* had sailed directly to New Zealand. It was Furneaux's Adventure Bay which they now sought in the knowledge that it would be a good place for wood and water.

The days were getting warmer and the thermometer was recording temperatures in the sixties Fahrenheit. A gentle breeze came from the south and took the ships into Adventure Bay. The *Discovery* arrived nearly two hours ahead of the *Resolution*, this was in spite of the fact that she was two or three miles to leeward during the night. Captain Clerke went on shore to examine the place; he found that water and wood were both plentiful but he was concerned about grazing for the cattle. There was a little grass but it was very coarse. The smoke from a single fire was seen in a valley about a mile from the shore, the smoke seemed to increase soon after the ships anchored which possibly meant that the Tasmanians had seen them arrive and had them under observation. The next day was spent in procuring wood and water and cutting what grass they could find for the cattle. In the evening they hauled in the nets and found they had caught more than enough fish to serve the ships' company. There were elephant fish, some small white bream, and an edible round flat fish which none of them had ever seen before.

At about four in the afternoon of the next day the Tasmanians decided to show themselves. Nine men appeared unexpectedly at the place where the sailors were cutting wood. The foremost man had something which looked like a spear in his hand and he held it in a striking position, but one of his companions made signs for him to drop it. William Anderson described the appearance of the indigenous Tasmanians:

These people were quite naked and destitute even of every ornament, though all unciviliz'd nations are fond of them, if we except a feather which one of them had in each side of his head and a bit of cord which one or two more had about their necks. They are of a middling size or rather smaller than most Indian nations: their colour is a dull black and not quite so deep as that of the African Negroes. Their hair however is perfectly wooly though something harsher than that of the last mentioned people, and it is clotted or divided into small parcels, either naturally as that of the Hottentots or with the use of some sort of grease mix'd with a red paint or ochre which they smear in great abundance over their heads: but least this might be the occasion of the frizzling disposition of the hair I examin'd a Boy narrowly who appear'd never to have us'd any & found it to be the same. Their features are not at all disagreeable, and their noses though broad or full are not flat and their lips of an ordinary thickness. The lower part of the face projects a good deal, as is the case in most Indians I have seen, so that a line let fall from the forehead would cut off a much larger portion than in Europeans. Their Eyes are of a middling size with the white less clear than in us, nor are they remarkably quick or piercing, but give a frank chearfull cast to the whole countenance. Their teeth are broad but not equal or well set, and either naturally or from dirt

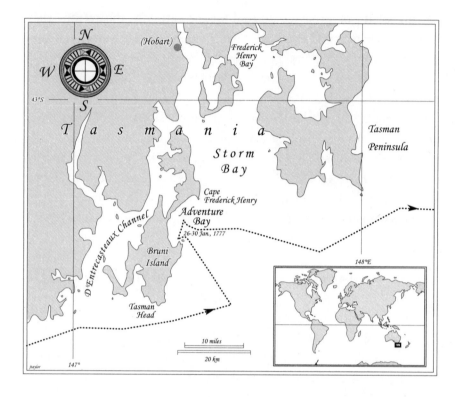

not of so clear a white as is usual amongst people of a black colour. Their mouths are rather wide but this appearance seems heighten'd by wearing their beards long and clotted with paint in the same manner as the hair of the head. In other respects they are well proportion'd though the belly seems rather projecting, which may be owing to the want of compression which most nations use more or less...[3]

The first two Tasmanians advanced from the edge of the wood and the rest soon followed. They did not seem to show any surprise at meeting another race of men, or at the strange objects such as the guns and saws which they had never seen before, but this may have been because they had been watching for several days from the cover of the woods. They soon became pretty familiar. They were offered knives and handkerchiefs after which they pointed and asked for anything which took their fancy. When they were denied they accepted the refusal and they did not seem disappointed. One or two tried to pilfer but when it came to theft they were nothing like as skilled as the Tahitians. They seemed not to understand the Polynesian language but they immediately repeated the word 'kangaroo'. The number of British who had seen a kangaroo was limited to the veterans of the *Endeavour* but this was one of the factors which confirmed Cook in his opinion that they had landed on the southernmost coast of New Holland.

The Tasmanian spears were blunt pointed instruments about 2 feet long. They were coerced into throwing them at a target so that the British could see how accurate they were, but the throwers were invariably wide of the mark. The British put up a piece of wood and made signs that they intended to fire at it with a musket. The report of the musket alarmed the Tasmanians so much that their new knives and hatchets were dropped on the ground as they scampered hastily back towards their habitation.

William Anderson thought them a mild and cheerful people with no reserve or jealousy of strangers. He put this down to a result of their poverty for they had no property or valuables to lose. Anderson had visited Easter Island and New Caledonia. Both these places were remarkable for their poverty and the people were quiet and indeed glad to see strangers come amongst them. He was unable to discover what they ate for food, they rejected the bread they were offered and they were revolted by the elephant fish which had been caught in the bay. They were seen to catch and eat birds and it was obvious from the shells that they dined on oysters, mussels and other shellfish.

In the bay were several primitive huts which seemed to have been built only for temporary purposes. Many of the largest trees had their trunks hollowed out by fire to a height of 6 or 7 feet, there were hearths made of clay in the middle of the hollows, with room for four or five people to sit round inside. The hollow trees were durable in that the natives took care to leave one side of the tree sound so that it still lived and seemed to grow as well as the trees which remained untouched. The Tasmanians mutilated themselves by cutting their skin with flints or sharp shells and rubbing ashes into the wound. Anderson thought little of their artefacts and social organisation:

> With respect to personal activity or genius we can say but little of either. They do not seem [to] posess the first in any remarkable degree, and as for the last they have to appearance less than even the half animated inhabitants of Terra del Fuego, who have not invention sufficient to make cloathing to defend themselves from the rigour of their climate though furnish'd with the materials. The small stick rudely pointed which we have already mentiond was the only thing we saw which requires any mechanical exertion, if we except some bits of Kangooras skin fix'd on their feet with thongs as amongst some labourers of other countrys; though it could not be learnt whether these were in use as shoes or only to defend some sore on the feet. They were even ignorant of the use of fish hooks, if we might judge from their being unable to comprehend the use of some of ours which were shown them, and indeed their indifference for the things we gave them & their general inattention were sufficient proofs of this defi- ciency.[4]

The weather was very sultry and calm. Cook was pleased to find a small island they named Penguin Island where there was an excellent supply of grass for the cattle. A group of inquisitive Tasmanians appeared and the captain went on shore to give them some trinkets, red baize cloth and other things which they accepted but they did not appear overjoyed. Seven or eight women arrived, some with children and some carrying striplings. They seemed to have a lighter skin than the men, and their hair was shorn off close except for a ring round the head 'exactly after the manner of Friars in Catholic countries'. Their only covering was a piece of kangaroo skin fastened about the shoul- ders and on the belly, and this seemed to be worn only to support their children on their backs for it did not cover those parts which most nations conceal.

There was no stigma about covering the private parts of either sex and the ship's surgeon was very specific about this, he had been on Cook's second voyage and he was quite experienced with the habits of primitive races:

> The men amongst the great Cyclades and at new Caledonia indeed cover the Penis but leave the Scrotum expos'd. Several of those in the last place even neglect covering the penis and go entirely naked. Add to this that the women suffer'd every part to be examined without the least appearance of bashfulness, and the men absolutely play with their penis as a child would with any bauble or man would twirl about the key of his watch while conversing with you. Their manner of making the natural Evacuations also show that they are either destitute of all sense of shame or at least that they are under no restraint amongst each other, for the men never chang'd their posture on making water and would sometimes not even move their legs out of the way but would suffer the Urine to run down upon them.[5]

James Burney witnessed the same scene, or something very similar to it, and he compared it to the action of a dog passing water:

> ...in the most natural actions they are without restraint, and have much less idea of decency than an English dog, who will lift his leg up, by which you may guess what he is going about; but one of these Gentlemen, whether sitting, walking or talking, will pour forth his streams without any preparatory action or guidance, or even appearing sencible of what he is doing; and not in the least interested in whether it trickles down his thighs or sprinkles the person next to him.[6]

As the Tasmanians became bolder they were prepared to accept gifts from the newcomers and Cook gave them some beads and other trifles which he had in his pocket. On this occasion he wore a striped jacket to which one of the men took a liking, and he readily gave the jacket to the admirer. It was good psychology for it pleased all of them greatly.

Others gave gifts so that all the Tasmanians received something and soon everybody was sociable and friendly. The Tasmanians were interested in the large crosscut saw which the carpenters used to shape parts for repairing the ship and after some instruction they were able to work the saw themselves. On their way to their habitations they passed the ship's watering place where the mate and six men were filling water casks.

> When our people saw the Indians coming they all run to the boat as they had neglected to carry any arms on shore out of the boat, not expecting any Indians. The Indians perceived that our people was frighted, began to jump and halloo, & even run to the Boat and endeavouring to hawl it on shore, but on firing a Musquet they all fled to the woods holding their fingers in their Ears: & we saw no more of them that evening — [7]

According to the ship's astronomer, William Bayly, there were some attempts to copulate with the native women, who ran around naked as we have observed. The chief allowed the women to stay for about an hour but when he realised the intentions of some of the seamen he sent them away. The Tasmanians returned the favour by mistaking the younger men, presumably those who had yet to grow a beard, as women. It was hardly surprising that no intercourse of any kind took place, the young men ran a mile from the vile smelling Tasmanian bodies with the lice hanging about their necks and other parts of their bodies.

It was January, Cook stayed only four days in Van Dieman's Land and on 30 January the ships were on their way again. As they sailed from Van Dieman's Land the expedition had reached the Pacific Ocean at last, but the world's greatest ocean is thousands of leagues across and it would take many months to get from the extreme south west to the extreme north east. Cook wanted to make one more port of call before heading for the tropical islands to the north and his next stopping place was New Zealand. If he had had time to spare then he would have mapped and charted the coast of Tasmania and sailed as far north as the latitude where the *Endeavour* had first sighted Australia. He believed that he had landed in Australia and that the coast was continuous all the way to Cape York. He missed the opportunity of discovering the Bass Straits between the Australian mainland and Tasmania. Tobias Furneaux had been in the same position four years earlier and Cook had accepted Furneaux's findings that Tasmania was part of the mainland. It was out of character for Cook not to take the opportunity to map and chart such an important landfall and the reason may have been that he still hoped to reach the north Pacific by the middle of the summer in the northern hemisphere. There was however, some unfinished business in New Zealand and the two ships set a course to the east.

On 10 February land was seen and identified as Rocks Point on the north coast of New Zealand's South Island. A few hours later Cape Farewell was sighted, an emotional headland named by Cook on the *Endeavour* voyage. It was the last point of New Zealand to be seen by the men of the *Endeavour* when they departed from that land. It was the fifth time Cook had visited New Zealand. On his first visit with the *Endeavour* he had spent many months circumnavigating and charting the North and South Islands. On his second voyage he had made three visits in all. He had used Queen Charlotte Sound as a base for the exploration of the extreme South Pacific in search of the southern continent. It was a voyage of terrible hardship as his ship followed the ice edge of the Antarctic seas. His consort on the second voyage, the *Adventure* commanded by Captain Tobias Furneaux, became separated by a storm and Furneaux arrived at the rendezvous too late to sail to the south with Cook. On his last visit to Queen Charlotte Sound Cook discovered that there had been a terrible tragedy and that ten of the crew of the *Adventure* had been murdered in a place called Grass Cove, which the sailors had rechristened Bloody Cove. The killing was even worse than murder, the evidence showed that the bodies of the men had been hacked to pieces and that the Maoris, who were well known to be cannibals, had eaten their flesh. James Burney had been a lieu-

tenant on the *Adventure* and he had been in charge of the search party
which found the mutilated bodies of the men. It was such a horrific
experience that for the rest of his life he could only speak of the incident in whispers. The British were not the only nation to suffer at the
hands of the Maoris, in 1772 there had been an incident at the Bay of
Islands when Marion du Fresne was slain with a number of his men.
For those prepared to go back to the previous century there was the
loss of life on Tasman's voyage when he named the place where he first
landed in New Zealand as Murderers Bay.

The Maoris could not miss the two ships entering the straits
between the North and South Islands. They had seen the *Resolution*
several times before. They knew that this was the white man, Captain
Cook coming back again to see them. What they did not know was why
he had come back. Was it to trade? Was it to water his ship and collect
plants and insects? Was it to extract retribution for the loss of his men?
They were very apprehensive about approaching the ship.

Cook began to set up camp onshore. William Bayly was able to set
up his observatory on the same spot he had used on his previous visit.
Bayly hardly needed to check the longitude, it had been measured from
this point many times before but he did want to know the error in the
ship's chronometer and this proved to be only a matter of a few
seconds. Cook posted a guard on the encampment. He could see the
remains of an English vegetable garden surviving from his last visit, it
was totally over-run with weeds but there were cabbage, onions, leeks,
parsley, radishes, mustard and a few potatoes to be found.

It soon became evident to the Maoris that Cook was not here to
take revenge, so they began to approach the encampment and trade
was quickly established. On 16 February at the break of day Cook set
out with a party of five boats to collect grass for the cattle. They soon
filled the boats and the party went on to Grass Cove where the
massacre had taken place in 1774. There they found an old Maori called
Pedro whom Cook had befriended on his previous visit. Cook was
anxious to get as near as he could to the truth of the incident. With the
help of Omai, who understood the language better than any of the

British, he was able to establish Pedro's account of the incident:

> ... Omai put several questions to Pedro and those about him on that head, all of which they answered without reserve, and like people who are under no apprehension of punishment for a crime they are not guilty of, for we already knew that none of these people had any hand in this unhappy affair. They told us that while our people were at victuals with several of the natives about them some of the latter stole or snatched from them bread, & fish for which they were beat this being resented a quarrel insued, in which two of the Natives were shot dead, by the only two Muskets that were fired, for before they had time to discharge a third or load those that were fired they were all siezed and knocked on the head. They pointed to the place of the Sun when this happened.[8]

The accounts varied a little in detail but Cook knew he had got close to the truth. The account written by James Burney is very similar:

> ... of this accident, the best account I have been able to gather, is, that our people were dining on the beach: during their meal, a Zealander stole something out of the boat, and was making off with it, on which Mr Rowe fired and killed the Thief on the spot. The Zealanders immediately sallied out of the Woods and got between our people and the boat, they say Rowe fired twice and killed another man, but the people's muskets had been left in the boat, nobody but himself having any firearms, so that they were easily overpowered and fell from imagining themselves too secure.[9]

The only positive thing to come out of the investigation was that the massacre was the result of a quarrel and it was not planned or premeditated. It came out that the leader of the Maoris on that occasion was a man called Kahourah who was still at large but was keeping his distance from the ships. When Kahourah discovered that Cook was not out for vengeance he grew bolder. Omai was easily able to identify him

and he even managed to get him on board the *Resolution*. Omai expected
Cook to take his revenge on Kahourah, so too did the Maoris and if
Cook had chosen to kill the man for his crimes they would have readily
accepted his vengeance:

> Omai was the first who acquainted me with his coming and desired to
> know if he should ask him on board. I told him he might and accord-
> ingly he interduced him into the Cabbin, saying 'there is Kahourah kill
> him' but as if he would have no hand in it himself, retired immidiately,
> but returned again in a short time and seeing the chief unhurt, said
> 'why do not you kill him, you tell me if a man kills an other in England
> he is hanged for it, this Man has killed ten and yet you will not kill
> him, tho a great many of his countrymen desire it and it would be very
> good'.[10]

Cook had to admit that what Omai said was true. Kahourah was
evidently very unpopular with his people, the Maoris knew what had
happened and if Cook killed the man there would be no retribution.
Cook had the man responsible for the slaughter in his power and before
him in his cabin. He asked the direct question of Kahourah, was he the
man responsible for the slaughter at Grass Cove?

> ...at this Question he folded his arms hung down his head and looked
> like one caught in a trap; And I firmly believe expected every moment
> to be his last, but was no sooner assured of his safety than he became
> cheerfull, yet did not seem willing to answer the question that had
> been put to him, till I had again and again assured him he should not
> be hurt. Then he ventured to tell us, that on offering a stone hatchet
> for sale to one of the people, he kept it and would give nothing in
> return, on which they snatched from them some bread while they were
> at victuals. The remainder of his account of this unhappy affair
> differed very little from what we had been told by other people, but
> the story of the Hatchet was certainly invented by Kahourah to make
> the English appear the first agressors.[11]

Thus Cook had finally decided not to take his revenge. It was not in his nature to take a life in cold blood and he could not see what would be gained by it. But there was little doubt that the Maoris did not respect his decision, they saw it as a weakness. Burney, who knew as much as anybody about the incident, refers to it in his journal along with other comments about the trade and attitudes of some of the Maoris:

> The New Zealanders of Charlotte Sound were never so much amongst us as this time: the reason probably, because they found more was to be got and on easier terms than ever before, for our folks were all so eager after curiosities and withal so much better provided than in any former voyage, that traffick was greatly altered in favour of the Indians: a Nail last Voyage purchasing more than an Axe or a Hatchet now. before our departure they carried Hatchets under their Cloaths instead of the Patoo. they often appeared to have a great deal of friendship for us, speaking sometimes in the most tender, compassionate tone of voice imaginable: but it not a little disgusted one to find all this show of fondness interested and that it constantly ended in begging, if gratified with their first demand they would immediately fancy something else, thier expectations and importunities increasing in proportion as they had been indulged. we had instances of their quarrelling after having begged 3 things because a fourth was denied them — it seemed evident that many of them held us in great contempt and I believe chiefly on account of our not revenging the affair of Grass Cove, so contrary to the principles by which they would have been actuated in the like case. another cause might be, thier getting from us so many valuable things, for which they regarded us as dupes to their superior cunning. As an instance how little they stood in fear of us, one man did not scruple to acknowledge his being present and assisting at the killing and eating the *Adventure*'s people.— [12]

Cook wanted to leave some of his domestic animals in New Zealand. He presented two goats to one of the chiefs, a male and pregnant

female. He gave two pigs, a boar and a sow, to another local chief. He
extracted promises that they would care for the animals and use them
for breeding and not kill them for food, but he did not have great faith
in their promises. At one time he had plans for leaving a bull and a cow
but he knew that there was no chief strong enough to protect them
and that they would not survive.

There was no reason to delay any longer in New Zealand, but there
was one more problem to be addressed before departure. Omai had
befriended one of the Maoris, a boy of about seventeen called Tiaroo.
He wanted his friend to sail with him to his home island. Cook was
reluctant to take Tiaroo because his mother was a widow and there was
no way he could ever get the son back home again. After some pres-
sure Cook gave in to the pleadings and he witnessed the sad and final
parting of a youth and his mother, both knowing that they would
never see each other again. But this was not all. On the day of departure a small boy of about ten was presented, to sail with Tiaroo to
Tahiti as a servant of Omai. Again Cook gave in, but the situation
seemed to be very different, there was no mother involved and the
boy's father presented him, 'With less indifference than he would have
parted with his dog'.

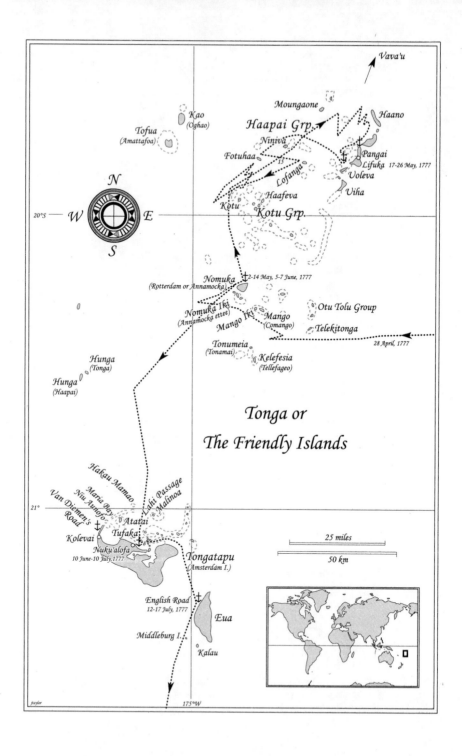

Vava'u

Moungaone   Haano

Kao
(Oghao)

Tofua   Haapai Grp.
(Amattafoa)
                    Niniva
        Fotuhaa   Pangai
                    15   Lifuka   17-26 May, 1777
                    Lofanga   Voleva
                                  Viha
        Kotu   Haafeva
                Kotu Grp.

N
W   E
S

20°S

Nomuka   2-14 May, 5-7 June, 1777
(Rotterdam or Annamocka)

        Nomuka Iki   Otu Tolu Group
        (Annamocka ettee)
                Mango Iki   Mango
                            (Comango)   Telekitonga

        Tonumeia   28 April, 1777
        (Tonamai)   Kelefesia
                    (Tellefageo)

Hunga   Tonga or
(Tonga)
                   The Friendly Islands
Hunga
(Haapai)

Hakau Mamao
                    Lahi Passage
Maria Bay
Niu Aunofo   Malinoa
Van Diemen's
Road   Atatai
Kolevai   Tufaka
        Nuku'alofa
        10 June-10 July, 1777
                    Tongatapu
                    (Amsterdam I.)

        English Road
        12-17 July, 1777
                    Eua
Middleburg I.
                Kalau

25 miles

50 km

21°

175°W

jtaylor

FIVE

The Tonga Islands

On the last day of February the ships had cleared the Cook Strait. The straits between the North and South Islands of New Zealand were named after their commander in 1770 on the *Endeavour* voyage, at the insistence of Joseph Banks. By 1 March the ships were in the open sea but heavy weather lay ahead of them. The two New Zealanders were not suffering from being homesick, they were suffering from being seasick, they sat on the decks holding their heads in their hands, moaning to themselves and singing doleful songs. Even the offer of a red cloak did nothing to take away their misery. On the majority of days the seas were heavy with the winds blowing hard from the wrong direction, between times there were milder spells but with hardly a puff of wind to move the ship. Some progress was made, but it was northwards towards the tropics rather than the direct course to Tahiti which required a more westerly course. After nearly a month at sea a small island was sighted, it was Mangaia in the Tonga Isles, part of a group which became known as the Lower Cook Islands.

Cook knew by this time that his chances of reaching the north Pacific for an attempt at the North West Passage in the coming summer had evaporated. He decided that he might as well explore the Tonga Islands, map and chart them and discover what he could of their culture. Four years ago, on his second voyage, he had passed through these islands with this same ship the *Resolution* in the company of the *Adventure*. A year later he had passed through them a second time with just a single ship, and the veterans of the second voyage had therefore landed on some of the islands before. He knew there were many islands in the group that he had not seen, and he also knew that the majority of them had never been visited by a European ship.

For once in his life there was plenty of time to spare. The ships cruised from island to island enjoying the blue seas and the open skies, plotting and charting, joining in with the local customs and in many cases making valuable records of a Polynesian society which had yet to be changed by contact with the outside world. They sailed from Mangaia to Atiu, on to Takutea, and then to the islands of Hervey and Palmerston which had been named by Cook on his second voyage. They spent two weeks on the island of Nomuke and from there they visited the Haapai group. They returned again to Namuke and sailed thence to Tongatapu, the island discovered by Abel Tasman in the seventeenth century and named by him Amsterdam.

There were more than 150 islands in the group. The breaking surf ran high and white where the sea broke on the idyllic beaches. But these were dangerous waters. Practically every island had a reef of sharp coral around it and if the sea carried a ship onto the reef the result would be torn sheathing and almost certain disaster. The harbours all had hidden rocks just below the surface, and the beaches had hidden sandbanks which were not visible at high tide. There were complex tidal currents in unexpected places. The *Discovery* lost her anchor when it was caught by a rock under the water, it was eventually grappled and recovered. Only the larger islands were inhabited but they were surrounded by many smaller rocky islands, which were difficult to see at night and were waiting to spell disaster to the ships. The safest course was to travel only during the daylight, to keep a lookout on the mast stationed at all times and in particularly dangerous conditions to send a boat ahead of the ships to sound the depth and to look for obstacles. The two ships remained some distance apart so that if an accident befell one of them then the other ship could send out the boats to the rescue. It was usually the smaller ship, the *Discovery*, which led the way, this was not because she was the more expendable of the two but because she was better than the *Resolution* at clawing off a lee shore and she could also sail in shallower water.

Some of the supplies were very low. Fresh water and wood were always needed. The latter was not for heating the ship as they were in the tropics and the thermometer was soaring, it was to fuel the still which was in use almost continually to create fresh water by boiling and distilling sea water. At one point the heavens opened and there followed a few days of rain. This was a blessing, the still could be stopped and the sheets were put out to collect rain water and to fill some of the barrels. Fresh meat and vegetables were always required but the trade in these commodities was good. The most urgent problem was food for the cattle, they were very short of hay and greens and an island with good pasture was urgently needed to feed them.

At the island known as Wennuate or Takutea grass was growing near the reef. The ship dared not go in too close and the crew had to wade along the reef knee deep through the water to carry the fodder to the boats. It was not until the ships reached the virgin island of Palmerston that they were able to set the cattle on land to enjoy a free grazing of scurvy grass, leaves and coconuts.

The Tongans were greatly excited to see the tall ships appear amongst them and they were very happy to trade. They exchanged breadfruit, plantains, yams, coconuts and sugar cane for nails and beads. They were a civilised arable people and most of these commodities were cultivated in well-ordered island plantations. The island pigs were in short supply and they could only be purchased with a knife or a hatchet, but wild fowl were plentiful and Cook managed to obtain all the supplies he needed. There was a little haggling on the exchanges but by and large the traders were honest. The real problem was the pilfering, the natives simply could not keep their thieving fingers off items made of metal, glass and even paper, to them these were strange and exotic materials which they had never seen before and which they desperately wanted to own for themselves. Everything removable had to be watched every second of the day and night but even the strictest precautions did not prevent valuable items from being stolen.

The first landing was at the island of Atiu where the landing party consisted of William Anderson, John Gore and James Burney with Omai included as interpreter. They were greeted by a chief who, as he welcomed them, was seated resplendently with large bunches of red feathers in his ears. When the landing party arrived he ordered his people to stand aside and about twenty young women appeared, ornamented with the same red feathers. The girls proceeded to perform a dance to a slow and serious air. Anderson was very taken with the beauty of the women, they all had dark hair which fell in ringlets down their neck, and the iris of their eyes also seemed jet black. When the dance came to an end there was a noise like the arrival of galloping horses. This sound turned out to be a party of men armed with clubs which they rattled against each other. The men proceeded to entertain their visitors with mock fights and dances using their clubs as accessories.

Omai discovered that the language was very similar to his native Tahitian but the dialect was different and he did have a few communication problems. When he saw that an oven was being prepared for food he became very agitated, he thought the ship had landed amongst cannibals and that the oven was being warmed up for the visitors to be, quite literally, part of the feast. Fortunately a large hog was spotted near the oven and his fears were proved unfounded. The Tongan dialect resembled the Maori language more than Tahitian so that the two Maoris were also valuable as interpreters, in fact the two spent most of their time with the Tongans and chose not to sleep on board the ship. They proved very popular, they showed off their Maori war dance to the great delight of the Tongans and they were asked to perform many encores.

News of the arrival of the two ships spread very quickly throughout the islands. This was hardly surprising considering that the only tall ships which had ever been seen were Cook's own vessels from four years earlier and Tasman's expedition which took place long before living memory, but was still preserved in the folklore. All the inhabited islands wanted the ships to call on them and they were all generous with their trade and entertainment. The visitors were given a great reception at the island of Nomuka. It was here that they met with Finau, the chief of the island who claimed to be king of all the islands in the Tongan group. A very grand reception was planned with the festivities starting in the afternoon and continuing well into the night. As the feasting began William Anderson noted two pigs and six fowl to his right, six pigs and two turtles to his left. This was only a fraction of the food available. It was a large gathering, nobody wanted to miss out on such a great occasion and the whole island was assembled. The artist John Webber painted the scene showing the musicians and dancers ordered in lines and circles with their audience a mass of faces arranged in a great arc many people deep.

The first entertainments were wrestling and boxing matches and the rules seemed to be very similar to the English rules, such as they were long before they were formulated by the Marquess of Queensberry. The wrestling bouts were very short and good-natured. James Burney gives us a brief description:

> They wrestle very much like our Cornishmen, and are very expert and active at it, when anyone was thrown, the victor was complimented with the following short song, in a kind of recitative, 'Tooway-Hey-O Mar to yoe' the meaning of which I am ignorant. The first word (Tooway) was sung by a single person, dwelling on the last syllable, and the rest in full chorus by the men on that side of the ring to which he belonged.[1]

The British were invited to take on the Tongans at wrestling, but Burney tells us that 'In wrestling with them our people were almost constantly worsted'. He goes on to give us more detail, including the reactions of the audience:

> ... the diversions and exercises of these people were conducted with a

degree of temper truly commendable, and which few are capable of; the conquerors not shewing any signs of exultation, nor the beaten party appearing in the least abashed, on the contrary, he returns to his Seat with as much unaffected chearfulness as when he entered the lists, it is not in the power of every man who suffers the disgrace of being worsted, to avoid feeling some degree of malevolence towards his antagonist, when any man advances and gives a general challenge, if another enters the lists whom he thinks too hard for him, or whom he does not chuse to encounter, he returns to his seat without being laughed at for his defection. during the whole of these exercises, the most perfect order was preserved, when engaged they used their utmost skill and strength: but if any thing like ill blood appeared between the combatants, the friends of either party interposed and seperated them immediately.[2]

There was an unexpected turn of events when two women ran out and entered the boxing arena. They were described by Thomas Edgar as 'two very fine Young Girls'. One of the midshipmen got up to try and separate the girls. This brought forth loud shouts of applause and a great deal of mirth amongst the spectators.

Captain Cook then allowed the marines to give the Tongans a demonstration of their firearms. The Tongans enjoyed the firing and the drilling but the marines were out of practice and the British thought they could have been far more professional and better disciplined. The Tongans responded with their own dance showing how they carried and hurled their clubs. This was a well-practised routine and it was certainly superior to the marines in terms of exactness, dexterity and timing. In the evening, when the sudden tropical darkness fell, when the fires glowed brighter and the stars came out, the marines were able to make up some of their lost ground and they gave a firework display with rockets and gunpowder. The Polynesians were astonished at the sight of the fires in the sky, there were great gasps of wonder from the audience, especially at some of the spectacular water rockets. They compared the sparks which fell from the rockets to falling stars, they were surprised at the height of the smoke column which remained behind after the rockets were spent and they conjectured that the smoke rose to become a cloud.

The musicians started to play. Some played a flute, rather like a pan pipe in construction, consisting of nine fistula blown through the nostril as opposed to the mouth. It was very similar to those seen on Tahiti but the music was different. The most common instrument was the native drum, they were made from tree trunks laboriously hollowed out with a slit just wide enough to put in a hand. The drummer held two sticks through the slit with which he beat the drum from the inside.

The evening progressed, with the palm trees, the ocean and the tropical skies as the scenery. It was a particularly memorable evening for the majority of the crew who had never been to the Pacific before. The food and drink flowed freely and the tempo of the drums caused all the hearts to throb in tune. The pipes and music built up the atmosphere. A band of eighteen musicians sat down in a circle at the place where the dances were to be performed. Four or five men carried large lengths of bamboo from three to six feet long, and they beat these poles constantly on the ground. All of them sang with a slow and soft air, which so tempered the harsher music that even those accustomed to hear the most perfect European music had to admit to the vast power and pleasing effect of this simple harmony. As the men sang the women arrived to dance:

> After continuing for about a quarter of an hour twenty women enter'd the circle most of whom had garlands of the crimson flowers of the China rose or others about their head, and many had cut some other leaves they had about them as ornaments with a great deal of nicety about the edges. They made a circle round the chorus turning their faces towards it, and began by singing a soft air to which responses were made by the chorus in the same tone, which were repeated alternately, during which time the women accompanied their song with several very gracefull motions of the hands towards the face and in

other directions, at the same time making constantly a step forward and then back again with one foot while the other was fix'd. They then turned their faces to the assembly, sung some time, and retreated slowly in a body to one part of the circle which was opposite to where some of the principle people sat as spectators in a small hut.[3]

The women broke into two columns and wove between each other in a passing sequence. The leaders advanced towards each other and stood in their station, the others advanced from each side in turn until they formed a perfect circle once more around the singers.

Their manner of dancing was now chang'd for a quicker sort in which they made a kind of half turn by leaping and clapp'd their hands, repeating some words in conjunction with the chorus, but towards the end as the quickness of the music increas'd they perform'd a sort of motion which with us would be rather reckon'd indecent, as they mov'd the lower part of the body on the trunk from side to side for a considerable time with such vigour and dexterity as shows they have been well initiated in the practice of it, on which they finish'd the dance.[4]

It was the men's turn to dance again. This time there were about fifteen men, some of them were elderly and seemed to have little agility for the dance. They were arranged in a circle divided at the front, with their faces turned inwards and they were accompanied by a musical chorus. Half the circle faced forwards as they advanced and the other half turned in the opposite direction. They sometimes sang slowly in conjunction with the chorus during which time they made very fine motions with their hands. The hand motions were different from those of the women, they inclined their bodies to either side alternately by raising one leg which was stretched outwards and resting on the other, the arm of the same side being also stretched fully upwards. At other times they recited sentences in a musical tone which were answered by the chorus, and at intervals increased the measure of their dance by clapping the hands and quickening the motions of their feet. At the end the music and dancing quickened in tempo, so much that it was hardly possible to distinguish the different motions. The whole lasted about half an hour.

The *pièce de résistance* was left until the end. These were the young and lascivious dancers, beautiful Tongan girls with flowers arranged in their dark hair, they were bare breasted and their dark bodies gleamed with perfumed coconut oil. John Williamson, third lieutenant of the *Resolution*, was something of a Puritan by nature but he gave the best description of this exotic dance:

> ... ever grateful for the civilities & Compliments shew'd them, [they] endeavour'd to amuse us for the reminder of the evening with a dance, by some of their dancing Women, who are early trained to it, for the entertainment of the great. [The principal Women who have at all times an Air of consequence & dignity in whatever they do, never perform among them] the dancers were upon this occasion particularly well dress'd after their manner, which consists of a large piece of their cloth of a brown colour, first doubled, & then with great exactness folded on the upper part into about thirty plaits, & tied with a kind of ribband made of the leaves of the plantin tree, dyed of different colours, round their waist, their hair is adorned with a variety of flowers, & the upper parts of the body rub'd over with a perfumed oil: from the stiffness of the cloth, its being plaited, & the manner it is put on, they look like persons just springing out of a cask; in these dances the Women have a variety of figures, all which they perform well, but with great labour to themselves: the custom of going with the upper part of their bodied naked is thought no way indecent, as the frequent view of the persons so expos'd rather checks than incites every loose appetite, to us the appearance of those women who had born many children was rather disgusting; but our ideas of disgust were soon changed to admiration when We beheld the most beautiful forms that imagination can conceive in the younger part of the Sex.[5]

The tropical night wore on. The drums beat faster and faster. They were entertained with more dancing. They were plied with more food and drink. Cook never discovered that it was all part of a very elaborate conspiracy. Finau and his henchman realised that they vastly outnumbered the British and they had evolved a plan for stealing the two ships and all their belongings. The authority for this comes from a man called William Mariner who lived amongst the Tongans many years later. It was not until 1806 that he heard the story, probably greatly embellished but basically true, from the son of Finau and from others who were involved. The idea was to get the whole of the crew onshore and to entertain them with a great feast. The marines in particular must be removed from the ships and this was why they specifically requested them to show their paces. This would leave the ships unguarded whilst the conspirators, with their great superiority in numbers, boarded and took the ships. For several hours, with Captain Cook totally oblivious to the danger, the expedition hung by a thread.

The coup never happened. If it had then Cook's third voyage would have been a very different story. The reason, according to Mariner's account, was an internal dispute between the plotters, some thought it best to take the ships in daylight, others thought the coup should be at night — they could not agree on this important point and consequently the coup did not take place at all. Cook and his men returned happily to the ship, many of them to enjoy the pleasures of the nubile South Sea maidens which literally cost them the shirt off their back, but none of them knowing how close they had come to disaster.

Then, on 27 May, came a surprise. Three large sailing canoes arrived at the island, they were the double hulled canoes which carried about fifty people each. In the leading canoe was a large and very obese man called Fatafeti Poulahu. When Poulahu landed Finau's regal behaviour underwent a significant change. It was obvious that Finau was not, as he had claimed, the supreme ruler of all the islands. He had overstated his importance, it was very obvious that he had to defer to Poulahu. 'If weight in body could give weight rank in rank or power', said William

Anderson, 'Poulaho was certainly the most eminent man in that respect we had seen, for though not very tall he was of monstrous size with fat which rendered him very unwieldy and almost shapeless.' Obesity was rare amongst the Polynesians, it needed high rank to be able to afford to consume so much food. The question of who was the real ruler of the Tongan Isles very soon became evident:

> This man's arrival sufficiently explain'd the behaviour of Feenou and points out his Character, for it seems to have been his aim all along to detain us amongst the islands where his authority was superior to those of every other person, and prevent us going to Amsterdam were he knew his true consequence must appear. His objections to our going there when at Annamooka, his directing us to Haapaee and the diligence he us'd there to procure us a sufficient supply are strong proofs of this; but finding us still bent on going there he not only set out for Va'vaoo to try if the things he could procure there would alter out purpose, but in all probability he had occasioned the report of a European ship being at Annamooka to be spread — perhaps with an intention of at least delaying our passage to Amsterdam by visiting that place, if not by the hopes that we might by lengthening our time meet with such bad weather as would oblige us to leave the islands intirely.[6]

The new arrival was from Tongatapu, the largest island in the group, and it now became obvious why the deceitful Finau had discouraged the British from sailing to Tongatapu. The newly discovered leader made Captain Cook a present of the highly valued red feathers and also a few hogs. Cook was able to give a length of printed linen cloth in return. Poulaho was invited into the captain's cabin. This created a problem for nobody was allowed to walk above the head of the great man, Cook had to clear the decks above the cabin and to post a guard so that no sailor could trespass there.

It was necessary to visit Poulaho's island of Tongatapu alias Amsterdam. The passage and the approach to the harbour were as

dangerous as any in the Tongan Isles, with very sharp rocks just below
the surface, but it was politically wise to accept the hospitality. Clerke
described the dangers of the coral rocks:

> We found this a most confounded navigation. The Bottom, which we
> too clearly saw a continued bed of Coral Rock, very uneven, with here
> and there a mischievous rascal towering his head above the rest, almost
> to the waters Edge; most providentially we had exceeding smooth
> water, with just such a breeze as we cou'd wish, and of course took
> every precaution we cou'd suggest, such as boats ahead, a good look
> out &c ; but these lofty Gentry's heads were so small that 'twas great
> odds but you miss'd them with the Lead in the boats, be as cautious as
> you wou'd. About 10 we gave one of them a rub but fortunately
> receiv'd not the least damage.[7]

The sequel to this visit was another round of Polynesian entertainment, wrestling, dancing and feasting and of course love making.
David Samwell, surgeon of the *Discovery*, described in his journal the
'Agee' girls or prostitutes of Tongatapu, and his journal also describes
something about the more respectable classes:

> The Women are in general handsome tho' many among them some-
> what masculine, & it was the general Opinion that in female softness
> & Delicacy they were excelled by the Otaheite Ladies, who from being
> more covered are of a fairer Complexion; however we saw great
> Numbers of Girls here as beautiful or more so than any at Otaheite &
> who in Symmetry & proportion might dispute the palm with any
> women under the Sun. They wear much the same kind of Clothing as
> the men & wear necklaces of Shells and the Legs of Fowls & some
> made of a small black Seed. They are clothed from the Waist to the
> Knees & all the other parts are exposed. The lower Class of young
> women have their Hair cut short, while those of the Agee order wear
> it long & flowing down their Shoulders which had a graceful and a
> truly elegant Appearance, & made us lament that the superstitious

Custom of mourning for the dead should deprive a young Creature as beautiful as Venus herself of her chief Ornament, which is always the Case on the Death of the Chiefs or their own Relations. As to modesty these women have no more Claim to it than the Otaheiteans, we have had on board the ships large Companies of them dancing stark naked, at the same time using the most lascivious Gestures. These Agee Girls, as we called them, never came on board the Ships, nor were their favours to be purchased for Hatchets or any thing else that we had, they are kept inviolate for the Chiefs who marry them. After lying in the women stain their bodies & faces of a yellow Colour & this they continue to do for a certain time. Polygamy seems to be allowed at these Islands to the Chiefs some of whom had four or five wives, tho' it is probable that none but those of the first Consequence are allowed as many, the generality of the people having only one.[8]

The dancing and the feasting were over. There was still plenty of time before sailing to the north but there had been the usual problem of thieving and it was not going to get any better the longer they stayed. Jackets and shoes had been lost, a dagger and a bayonet were stolen at Atiu, and there was also a close call when one of the muskets went missing. One of the thieves stole the bolt from the spun yarn winch, this was a machine for spinning yarn into ropes, it was useless without this essential part and the stolen item was useless on its own. Two of the ship's cats were stolen from the *Discovery*, this was not the sum total of the cats' complement but it caused great concern to Charles Clerke who feared that the rat population would quickly get out of hand without them. Edgar, the ship's master, noted that the cats were eventually returned but not before the thief had been put in irons. Three glasses were stolen from the astronomical quadrant. The ships' chronometers had to be guarded so carefully that the Tongans thought them to be gods, or at least the most sacred of holy relics. Clerke resorted to shaving the culprits when he could catch them, sometimes shaving only half of the face and head so they became objects of ridicule to their peers. Cook, when he was angry, resorted to his technique of capturing leaders and canoes, refusing to free them until the stolen items were returned. On his first voyage to the Pacific Cook used the lash on very few occasions and then only on his own men to keep discipline. On this voyage he used it on the Tongans, to set an example when he found them guilty of thieving, often giving three or four dozen lashes with sometimes as many as six dozen. It was out of character with the humane man who captained the *Endeavour*. It did not prevent the thefts. Samwell described an experience where one of the girls enticed him into a house for what he thought were sexual favours but which turned out to be an elaborate plan to rob him:

> ...as I had no Suspicion of the Snare that was laid for me I stopped for her, when she came up with me she desired me to return to the House & was sollicitous to keep me in discourse, making use of her female arts & blandishments, when I was all of a sudden seized hold of by the Indian from behind who held me fast while my fair Dalilah & the other young Indian fell a plundering my breeches pockets, but not being quite so expert at this business as those of the same profession in London they found it very difficult to get the beads out, on which I told the Indian that if he would loose my Hands I would give him everything I had quietly, after a little persuasion & observing the Trepidation the two young pickpockets were in & what a poor Hand they made of it, he consented, on which I instantly laid hold of a weapon I had about me, no other than a Hatchet & made a blow at him, but missed him; he endeavoured to lay hold of me again, but well knowing that putting a good face on the Matter would be the only way to extricate myself out of their Hands, I followed my blow & after making an Effort or two to lay hold of me he took to his Heels finding himself deserted by his Confederates, who had run away in the utmost precipitation on my first getting loose, I thus saved above one half of the Beads & probably my Cloaths which it is odds but they intended to take from me. This was the only instance of Violence that I met with among them, tho' I was frequently as much in their Power as I was at this time.[9]

There were other, even more disturbing aspects of the Tongan society. Samwell tells of a religious ceremony which took place annually and involved human sacrifice. The reason seemed to be for no better purpose than to force the populace to pay their respects to the chiefs of the islands and to show that they had an absolute power over their subjects. As many as fifty people were sacrificed. It was Finau who described the ritual to a horrified Samwell, he was very proud of the fact that he could sacrifice six victims, more than any other of the chiefs:

> And they told us that in about a Month's time another Festival was to be held in the same place on the like Occasion, at which the Chiefs were to do him Homage and acknowledge their Lives to be in his Hands, by each of them killing a certain Number of their dependents in his Presence, & they said that about 50 human Sacrifices would be offered up on the occasion; Pheenow was to kill the greatest Number of any of the Chiefs, his Quota being six, the rest were to slay some four, some 3 & others two & one according to their different Ranks. This horrid business was to be performed by the Chiefs themselves who knock the Victims in the Head with a Club. We asked them if those who were to be sacrificed knew that they were to be the Victims; they told us not & that if they did they would run away, but that they were always taken unawares. Such is the Savage Custom of these People, & in such a deplorable state of Servitude do the lower Rank of men live among them that they hold their existence but at the will of their Masters.[10]

Cook's patience was under great strain towards the end of the visit. The pilfering was a very annoying problem on top of the problems of water and supplies. But the ships managed to depart on good terms with presents exchanged all round. Poulaho was given a bull and a cow with instructions for keeping them healthy. Finau, in spite of his deceit, was given a horse and a mare but if the full details of his

conspiracy to capture the ships had been known then he would probably have been put in irons. Mareewagee, a lesser chief at Tongatapu,
was given a ram and two ewes to care for.

There was no hurry to move on so Cook waited for the eclipse of
the sun on 5 July, it would give a useful check on the longitude calcula-
tions. He was disappointed for even in the tropics astronomical events
can be thwarted by cloud. On 10 July the *Resolution* and *Discovery* set sail
for Tahiti.

The Tongans knew that there were other islands to the east and the
west, but they were very distant and there was no trade or traffic
between them. They were isolated from the Tahiti group. There was
an interesting incident at the Tonga Islands however, a group a
Tahitians appeared by accident, they had been blown many miles to
the west by storms and contrary winds until they had accidentally and
very fortuitously found themselves in the Tongan group of islands. It
showed that the distances between the Polynesian island groups of the
Pacific could be crossed with their own canoes, albeit by storm and
accident and it provided a valuable clue as to how the language and
customs of the islands came to have so much in common.

SIX

Tahiti and Beyond

On 29 July, just as darkness had fallen, there was a sudden squall of wind. It was so strong that both ships suffered some damage. The *Resolution* escaped with two torn sails but the *Discovery* was worse hit, she was laid right down on her beam ends and the stresses caused serious damage to her main mast. The main top mast snapped clean off just above the footing and there was another breakage about 3 feet below the cross trees. As the top mast fell it brought the top gallant sail and all the rigging with it and the yard arm which carried the sail was also broken. Two seamen were injured, the sudden lurch of the ship caused one to be thrown down the fore hatch, the other was dashed against one of the ship's boats which were firmly lashed down on the decks. The fall of the top mast created a chaos of ropes and rigging with sails from both the fore mast and the mizzen mast damaged by the fall. John Martin, a midshipman who was on watch at the time, described the scene:

> This squall, that did us so much damage, came on so suddenly & so violently, & the ship lay along in such a manner, that I who had the watch off deck, was obliged to haul myself up the ladder, on getting above deck the Scene was horrid, the wreck of the broken mast hanging over the Side, the night so very dark and Raining & blowing

Extreamly hard, Lost sight of our consort, so that everything seemd
to add to our distress, youth, health and good will, got the better of
these Difficulties, & by 12 of the night all but the Watch were Sufferd
to go below.[1]

The damage was caused by a freak gust of wind and the storm did not
last long. Luckily the ship could still make reasonable progress with
the remaining masts and sails but the major repairs would have to wait
until they had a good anchorage. About three days later a small inhabited island was seen. It was the island of Tubuai in the Austral Group,
the inhabitants waved and beckoned to the ships to stop but they were
only about three days from Tahiti and Cook did not want any delays.
He chose to sail on. It was 12 August when the high volcanic peaks of
Tahiti appeared in the mist above the horizon.

Tahiti can be described as two islands joined together by a narrow
isthmus, and as Cook was approaching from the south he chose to
anchor at Vaitephia Bay on the southern 'island' which is called
Taiarapu. As soon as the ships had been spotted, the Tahitian canoes
came out to trade and the Europeans received the usual tumultuous
reception from the excitable inhabitants. In one of the canoes there
were cries of a woman who appeared to be in great distress. She was
taken on board the ship weeping but her tears were not what they
appeared. They were tears of joy. She was the sister of Omai — her
brother had been absent from his country for so long. Omai embraced
his sister and he too burst into tears, brother and sister went below
decks embracing each other to hide their emotions.

The next news Cook discovered was that two Spanish ships from
Lima in Peru had been at Tahiti after he left in 1774 and they had
stayed for a long time, for about a year. The Spaniards were evidently
still keen to claim their Papal rights over all discoveries in the Pacific
Ocean, so much so that by all accounts they had extorted a promise
from the islands' chiefs that they would never trade again with the
English. Luckily for Cook's expedition the Tahitians needed very little
encouragement to forget their promises. The British were shown a

small house which the Spanish had built containing furniture and a cross. The cross carried the inscription 'Christus vincit Carolus III Imperat 1774' which to Cook's eyes looked rather like a Spanish claim to the discovery of Tahiti. Cook himself had been at Tahiti four times before the Spanish, Samuel Wallis with his ship the Dolphin had been there two years before Cook and the French had also been at Tahiti before the Spanish. On the other side of the cross Cook carved the legend 'Georgius Tertius Rex Annis 1767, 69, 73, 74 & 77'.

The Spanish had left behind a very fine bull, a bulky spirited beast. With their bullfighting tradition they had very good expertise in the breeding of bulls. 'A finer beast than he was I hardly ever saw', said Cook, who rarely used superlatives. The coming of the British proved to be a most fortunate event for the Spanish bull, three English heifers were released to keep him company. We may be sure that there were no language barriers between them!

After a few days in Vaitephia Cook wanted to sail on to his old familiar anchorage at Matavai Bay on the northern 'island' of Tahiti. He knew it to be a good anchorage and he also knew that he would meet there many of the people he had met on his previous visits. It also seemed the best place in Tahiti for the essential repairs to the main mast of the Discovery. The move was not a popular decision at Vaitephia, the residents were jealous of the honour which the great ships gave them and the trade which they brought. There was another problem in that the Tahitians, as was all too common, were in a state of civil war with each other and Cook had to sort out the complex politics and find out for himself who the current rulers of the island were.

'It was growing duskish as we went round Point Venus', wrote James King poetically. 'And entering Matavai Bay, about a hundred people were collect'd on the beach observing us with silent attention. Matavai Bay has a most picturesque appearance...'. The arrival was very unusual in that instead of great masses of canoes a single canoe came out to the ship to ask politely if they wanted to trade. Trade resumed the next morning. At Matavai Bay the new ruler was Otoo, also known as Otou or simply Tu, a man whom Cook knew from his previous visit in 1774. Otoo arrived amid great ceremony with a crowd of followers. The two peoples exchanged gifts and presents. The red feathered bonnets which the ships had brought with them from Tonga proved very popular, so much so that Cook was able to trade one feather bonnet for as many as ten large hogs. Captain Cook had brought along with him turkeys, geese, hens and ducks, also a peacock and a peahen, the special gift of Lord Bessborough. It was a curious twist for the English to be bringing such a brightly coloured species as a peacock to the topics. He also gave the Tahitians a horse and a mare, sheep and ewes and his one bull. The gifts were something of a relief for him, he was pleased to be freed of the responsibility of the large animals on the ship's deck for they needed a lot of space and a great deal of food.

Not least in importance was the return of Omai who, after all his amazing travels to the other side of the world, was back at last in his home country. Omai naturally expected his countrymen to treat him as a returning hero after his exploits in London and his meeting with the great white king. He was quickly disillusioned, but the reasons were partly his own fault. When Omai went forth to make an impression on his countrymen his dress sense left a little to be desired. 'On this occasion', said Cook, 'Omai, assisted by some of his friends, dressed himself not in English dress, nor in Otaheiti, nor in Tongatabu nor in the dress of any Country on Earth, but in a strange medley of all he was possess'd of.' When in London Omai had taken a fancy to a suit of armour which he had managed to purchase. It is impossible to conjecture anything more uncomfortable in the tropics but he still managed to wear a few pieces. Even James Burney, who had spent much time with Omai and had helped him in English society, had by this time also tired of his vanity. 'To say the truth', said Burney, 'Omaihs vanity and extravagance was but too great an encouragement to people of this stamp, he always went dressed in the most tawdry manner he could contrive and was consequently attended by a large train of followers whose only motive was to profit from his profusion and carelessness.' When the horses were unloaded from the ship to enjoy the freedom of a canter on land these noble beasts made a great impression on the

Tahitians. Cook and Clerke exercised the horses every day and rode them around the bay. The Tahitians were so amazed by the splendid creatures that they turned out daily to witness this event. Omai wanted to show off to his countrymen how well he could ride the horses. When he fell off it did nothing to improve his image!

Omai had been given his own articles of trade such as nails, beads and hatchets. Joseph Banks, with the best of intentions, had also given him an 'electrical machine'. Electricity was almost as mysterious to the Europeans as it was to the Tahitians and no details of this machine are available, but it was probably a device for building up electrostatic charge and inflicting minor electric shocks on unsuspecting people. William Bayly, the astronomer, mentions it amongst Omai's possessions:

> I cannot help remarking that those who had the care of fitting out Omi, used him exceeding ill, by giving him a collection of the worst things that could be procured. In the first place he had only 8 Spike-nails which seemed to have been put in by accident, the rest were all small rubbish that could not be of any manner of service to him either as trade or otherwise. His Hatchets were the very worst that are made for sale except 4 or 5 that might have cost a Shilling or 14d each in England, & among 20s worth of glass Beads there was not one that these people would give Cocoanuts for, or any thing else. Omi being a man of pleasure neglected to inspect into his own Afairs but left it entirely to other people. But when he came to examine the contents of his Boxes & Casks, he was very near going out of his Senses, finding himself little richer, either in knowledge or Treasure, than when he left his native country. Tho Mr Banks was considered as Omi's friend he did not give him a single hatchet or any thing else except A[n e]Lectrifying Machine which could be of no service to him had he known how to use it. This Omi declared to every body on board. But Omi was tolerable well furnished at last by exchanging with the officers of the Ships some of his useless things for usefull ones.[2]

According to Bayly, Cook planned to marry Omai to Otoo's youngest
sister, this would have given him a high status in Tahitian society. But
Omai discovered that the sister was already married, or at least she had
a male living with her. This man and his friends provided Omai with a
'very fine girl' as some form of compensation, but then they tried to
rob him of his belongings during the night. The girl was in on the
conspiracy, there was a great quarrel after which she left Omai after
stealing many of his things. To cap it all Omai claimed that she gave
him 'the foul disease'. This generated sympathy for poor Omai and as
a result Cook decided to change his plans, he thought it would be
better to try and find a suitable position for him on one of the other
islands.

At Matavai Bay Cook was pleased to meet a very pleasant young
man whom he knew from his previous voyage. The man was Odiddy, he
had sailed from Tahiti to New Zealand on the *Resolution* and he had
made the terrible cold voyage to the Antarctic when Cook had sailed
to a latitude of more than 70°. On that occasion the *Resolution* had
sailed to Easter Island and on to the Marquesas before returning to
Tahiti. Thus, unlike Omai, Odiddy was returned to his home and he
did not make the journey to England. James Cook gave his old friend a
chest of tools and other articles which greatly pleased Odiddy. Then
Cook gave instructions on how to lay out a garden with melons, potatoes, pineapples and two shaddock trees. Cook had great hopes that his
agricultural efforts would succeed and improve the living standards on
Tahiti. In fact nearly all his well-meaning experiments were a disaster,
William Bligh, master of the *Resolution* on Cook's voyage, returned to
Tahiti ten years later as captain of the *Bounty* on the infamous mutinous voyage. By that time the cows had produced eight calves and the
ewes had produced ten lambs but the turkeys and the peacocks had not
produced any young at all. When Bligh found the garden, nothing of
Cook's efforts remained except the two shaddock trees which had both
prospered and carried a fine harvest of fruit.

The two New Zealanders had grown accustomed to life on board
the ship and the arrangement was that they were to stay on Tahiti.

They were able to communicate quite well with the natives and they were very happy with the arrangement. Samwell's account of the Maori boys in Tahiti is the best, it ends with an amusing and sexually lewd version of ladies' football:

The two New Zealand boys spent much of their time on shore, being much delighted with the Beauty of the Island, & the people behaved in a friendly manner towards them, the young one Cocoa had a few Battles with the Otaheite Boys & was generally worsted by stripplings less than himself, which convinced him at last that it would be best to live in peace with them.

Cocoa being what we call an unlucky Dog was fond of playing his Tricks, which now & then would bring him into Squabbles with the Girls. One of these being plagued by him reproached him with his Countrymen eating human flesh, at the same time making signs of biting her own Arm, the poor boy was much hurt at it and fell a crying; but presently recovering out of his Confusion and being still insulted by her, he put his fingers to his head as if searching for a louse & made signs of eating it, at the same time telling her that if his Countrymen eat human flesh She eat lice which was almost as bad; by this quick stroke of retaliation our young Zealander got the laugh of his Side & the Girl was obliged to retreat & leave him master of the field. Tayweherooa the eldest boy always lived upon good terms with them & was esteemed for his friendly & modest disposition. The Otaheite Girls have a play which I dont remember to have seen noticed in the Accounts of former Voyages, by excelling in which they gain an extraordinary Pr[i]viledge, this is no other than a Game at football (the ball is a breadfruit) and she who comes off victorious has the Liberty of exposing her nakedness to the Croud about them & this right they are always sure of asserting.[3]

Samwell concluded with a story about Orettee, the chief who had been the friend of Bougainville when the latter was in Tahiti, he was the father of the Tahitian called Ohutoru who sailed on Bougainville's ship to France. Orettee came from a distant part of the island but took his abode at Matavai during the stay there. He was fond of talking of his son and of his friend Bougainville whom he called Orettee after himself, having changed names with him according to the custom of the country. Cook was very interested in Orettee's conversation about Bougainville, the two great explorers had never met each other and they had a great deal in common. According to Ellis Chief Orettee was on board the ship nearly every day, but he became something of a nuisance by always getting drunk.

Supplies of food were good and things were going well. Cook was invited to attend a peace thanksgiving ceremony at Attahourou but he was suffering from rheumatism and he had to decline the invitation. The next day, when news of his condition became known, a party of twelve women arrived at the ship. The party consisted of Otoo's mother, his three sisters and eight other women. It is well known that although Captain Cook allowed his men to enjoy the favours of the South Sea maidens he never indulged in the practice himself. But he tells us in his own journal what happened next. He was massaged by no less than twelve women. He obviously enjoyed it thoroughly but it was, of course, undertaken purely for medical reasons!

> At first I thought they came into my boat with no other view than to get a passage to Matavai, but when they got to the Ship they told me they were come to sleep on board and to cure me of the desorder that I complained of, which was a sort of Rheumatick pain in one side from my hip to the foot. This kind offer I excepted of, made them up a bed in the Cabbin floor and submited my self to their direction, I was desired to lay down in the Midst of them, then as many as could get round me began to squeeze me with both hands from head to foot, but more especially the part where the pain was, till they made bones crack and a perfect Mummy of my flesh — in short after being under their hands about a quarter of a hour I was glad to get away from them. However I found immediate relief from the operation, they gave me a nother rubing down before I went to bed and I found my self pretty

easy all the night after. They repeated the operation the next Morning before they went a shore, and again in the evening when they came on board, after which I found the pains intirely removed and the next Morning they left me. This they call Romy an operation which in my opi[ni]on far exceed[s] the flesh brush, or any thing we make use of of the kind. It is universally practiced among them, it is some times performed by the men but more generally by the Woman. If at any time one appear languid or tired and sit down by any of them they immeditely begin with Romy upon your legs, which I have always found to have an exceeding good effect.[4]

The cure implies that Cook may have been suffering from a trapped sciatic nerve which was freed by the massage. Soon afterwards Otoo appeared to say that the Tahitians were planning a great naval review at a place called Oparre. There were to be many canoes and Cook would be entertained with mock battles and Tahitian naval tactics. The review had been arranged for the benefit of the visitors and it would be churlish to refuse. Cook described the event in his journal:

I now went in my boat to take a view of them and to go with them to Oparre but soon after a Resolution was taken by the Cheifs not to go there till the next day. I looked upon this to be a good opportunity to get some insight into their Manner of fighting and desired Otoo to order some of them to go through the necessary manouvres. Two were accordingly ordered off, in one of them Otoo Mr King and my self went and Omai in the other. After we were out in the bay, we faced, and advanced upon each other and retreated by turns, as quick as the paddlers could move them; during this the wariors on the Stages flourished their weapons and played a hundred Antick tricks which could answer no other end that I could see than to work up their passions for fighting. Otoo stood by the side of the Stage and gave the necessary orders when to advance and when to retreat, in this great judgement and a quick eye combined together seemed necessary to seize every advantage that might offer and to avoide giving advantage. At last

after advancing and retreating, to and from each other at least a dozen
times, the two canoes closed, head to head, or stage to stage and after
a short conflict, the troops on our Stage were supposed to be killed and
we were board[ed] by Omai and his associates, and that very instant
Otoo and all the paddlers leaped over board to save their lives by
swiming.[5]

As soon as the mock fight was over, Omai put on his suit of armour,
mounted a stage in one of the canoes and was paddled all along the
shore of the bay. Everyone had a full view of him but he did not
manage to draw their attention so much as he expected.

It was all very entertaining but when the manoeuvres were all over
Omai explained that the naval engagements were not always conducted
in the same manner. He explained that they sometimes lashed the two
canoes together head to head and then they fought until all the
warriors were killed in either one or the other of the canoes. This
method of fighting was used when they were determined to conquer or
die, it was a bloody engagement and all agreed that they never give
quarter, unless it be to reserve them for an even more cruel death on
the next day.

Cook noted that the power and strength of the islands depended
entirely on their navies, he had never heard of any general engagement
which had been fought on land. The time and place of the naval battles
were fixed upon by both parties, the preceding day and night was spent
in feasting. In the morning they launch the canoes, they put everything
in order and on the next day begin the battle, the fate of which generally ends the dispute. The vanquished save themselves by a precipitate
flight from the battle and if they can reach the shore they fly with their
friends to the mountains, for the victors do not spare the old, the
women or the children. The next day they assemble at the Morai to
return thanks for the victory and to sacrifice the slain and prisoners if
they have any. After this a treaty is set on foot, the conquerors for the
most part obtain their own terms, by which lands and sometimes
whole islands change their owners. Omai told how he was once taken

prisoner by the men of Bolabola and carried to that island, where he and some others would have been put to death the next day had they not found means to make their escape during the night.

As a parting gift Cook had John Webber paint his portrait and he presented the portrait to Otoo. Bligh saw the portrait in 1788 when he landed with the *Bounty*, and later visitors to Tahiti also saw it. It seems not to have survived much longer however, for there are no reports of it in the nineteenth century. We do have a Webber portrait of Cook so we may assume that Otoo's portrait was very similar, but it is still a loss that the Tahiti portrait of Cook can no longer be seen.

The main mast of the *Discovery* was repaired and the ships were ready to go to sea. It was still only September and there seemed little to be gained by getting to the Northern Hemisphere before the spring. If Cook had known the truth about the North West Passage and the amount of exploration before him then he would certainly have left earlier. He decided instead to make a leisurely visit to the neighbouring island of Moorea which beckoned to him on the horizon and was only a few miles from Tahiti. In his three previous visits he had never been there, the main reason being that he thought there was no suitable harbour for his ships. In fact Moorea had an excellent sheltered harbour which lay hidden in the cone of an extinct volcano. It was almost totally enclosed by steep volcanic rocks but there were gaps between the rocks giving passage to the sea and there were several places where it was possible to land.

It was at Moorea that the problems began. Amongst many other wonders on the ship the islanders were fascinated by the goats, and one of them was stolen. It was returned the next day but a second goat was stolen immediately afterwards. Cook sent out two men to retrieve the animal but after a whole day the men returned empty handed. Cook was angry. He then made an uncharacteristic blunder and he set out with a strong armed party to retrieve the goat by force. Omai, who was always eager to give advice, suggested that he shoot every man whom they met on the way. Cook had more sense than to take this aggressive attitude but he did plunder across the island burning houses and destroying every canoe he could find. The goat was retrieved but only at a terrible cost in property and the loss of a great deal of goodwill.

The next problem was the theft of the sextant. This was a far more serious matter than the goat. Cook was tipped off by Omai, he had a good idea which man was the guilty party but the offender coolly denied that he had stolen the instrument. Omai knew the man was guilty however, and he cleverly wormed out a confession, even finding out where it had been hidden. Again Cook showed an uncharacteristic anger, he not only shaved the man's head but he cut off his ears in a desperate attempt to make an example of him in front of the other islanders. The thief took his revenge by destroying Omai's garden. This time Cook put him in irons on board the ship. The man managed to reach the drawer where the keys were kept, he unlocked his irons and escaped. Cook was so annoyed that Thomas Morris, the sentry on duty, was punished with twelve strokes of the lash on three successive days. William Harvey, who as the mate of the watch was partly responsible for the escape, was disrated to midshipman and transferred from the *Resolution* to the *Discovery*.

More harsh naval punishment was dealt out at Moorea than on the whole of the *Endeavour* voyage. The loss of a season had resulted in far too much free time and nearly all of it was spent in the exotic islands of the Pacific. It was far too long for the crew to be idle, but Cook himself was acting out of character. The many problems were wearing him down and when he had to solve them he had lost some of his humane side. Soon came the problem of the deserters. Some of the younger men were tasting the fruits of love for the first time and it was hardly surprising that friendships were struck up with the Tahitian girls. The first to desert was John Harrison, a very young man of sixteen who was a marine private on the *Resolution*. Then came Alexander Mouat and Thomas Shaw of the *Discovery*. Mouat's case was particularly disturbing, he was a young midshipman and his father had been a respected naval captain.

Cook had plenty of experience with this situation. There was no way he could turn a blind eye to it. He took the chiefs as hostages on board his ship — he treated them well but he refused to let them go until his men were returned. As usual, after a time the runaways were brought back to the ship.

There had been a dual at Matavai Bay which Cook did not record but the story is told by William Griffin, ship's cooper. John Williamson and Molesworth Phillips fought a duel with pistols. After two rounds had been fired neither man was wounded and the seconds persuaded the contestants that justice had been done and the duel should be abandoned. The duel is not mentioned in Cook's journal and he made no retribution on the guilty parties so it was probably kept from his ears.

Then came another blow. Just as the two ships were almost ready to leave on the next leg, William Anderson, the surgeon's mate on the *Resolution* and Charles Clerke, the captain of the *Discovery* both requested permission to stay at Tahiti until the following summer. Both were suffering from consumption and they felt unable to face the severe weather they would experience inside the Arctic Circle. They were both key men on the expedition. There is a minor mystery over Clerke's case, he had to get his papers in order before he could leave his ship. As the ships cruised from island to island there was plenty of time for him to work on his papers and to leave the competent and experienced John Gore in command of the ship. But Clerke never got his papers in order and the reason may have been that, unlike those who wished to stay for romantic reasons, he was undecided about the prospect of being left for an unspecified time on a Pacific island. Hopes of finding the North West Passage were still high and if the expedition proved to be successful then the men would have to be left for an indefinite time on Tahiti. For this and other reasons neither Clerke nor Anderson, in the final reckoning, opted to stay on Tahiti. It solved a problem for James Cook but it did not solve the problem of two terminally ill men on the expedition.

Cook was glad to be leaving at last for the main purpose of the voyage. The enforced stay of nearly a year in the tropics was necessary as they had to wait for the summer season to explore the northern seas.

The sailors loved the tropical islands and the attentions of the Polynesian girls and to them the thought of leaving to sail the coldest seas in the north was not a pleasant thought. Cook condoned the sexual relations but there remained a nagging doubt in his mind for they were frequently accompanied by venereal disease. There was an endemic form of the disease, known as the yaws, which had always been present in the Polynesian islands but there was little doubt that all the contact with the European ships was causing the spread of venereal disease to the islands. Cook was unable to prevent the intercourse but he laid down strict rules for hygiene and he held regular medical inspections. The importance of cleanliness and hygiene were well understood, but the state of an eighteenth-century sailing ship after eighteen months at sea can only be imagined. On 31 Oct Cook put as much of the stores ashore as he could so that the cockroach problem could be tackled. The ship was smoked with gunpowder and immense numbers were killed. 'These insects were so innumerable on board the *Resolution* that they run in every part of her so thick you would think the ship alive, even the closest box or trunk were all alive with them and they eat and destroy every thing they have' (Bayly). There was a great blitz on the cockroaches, they were crawling everywhere around the ship, but it did very little to reduce their numbers. When the ships moored at Moorea the distance from ship to shore was only about 30 yards and a bridge was created from one of the hawsers so that the rats could run ashore from the hold of the ship. Some took advantage of the situation and escaped to the tropical island, but the majority chose to sail with Captain Cook and to live off the foodstuff stored in the hold. There was no chance of containing the venereal disease in these filthy conditions.

On Sunday 2 December there was a favourable wind and at four in the afternoon the ships sailed from the harbour of Raiaitea. Many local people were still on board but they were able to leave using their canoes. There was a minor hitch when a hawser was cut by a sharp rock and Cook had to send a boat to retrieve it. The last to leave the ship was Omai, he was glad to be back in his home country but his great adventure had come to an end and he expressed great emotion at seeing his friends for the last time:

> Omai took his leave of us with manly sorrow, until he came to Captn Cook when with all ye eloquence of sincerity he express'd his gratitude and burst into tears. The Captn who was extremely attentive to Omai ye whole time of his being on board, & ye pains he had taken to settle him to his satisfaction in his native country, was much affected a this parting. Omai too late saw his error & often wish'd himself in England again, saying, his time should be spent in learning what would be useful to him instead of throwing his time away at cards, however sincere Omai might be at this time, I believe had he gone to England again (which was greatly his wish and desire) he would have acted the same part over again being extremely fond of a gay Life & being thought a great man.[6]

The two Maori boys were also in tears at the parting. Twice, as they were being taken from the ship in the canoes, they jumped overboard. Twice they swam back to the ship. Eventually they had to be held down by force in the canoes to make them stay at Tahiti.

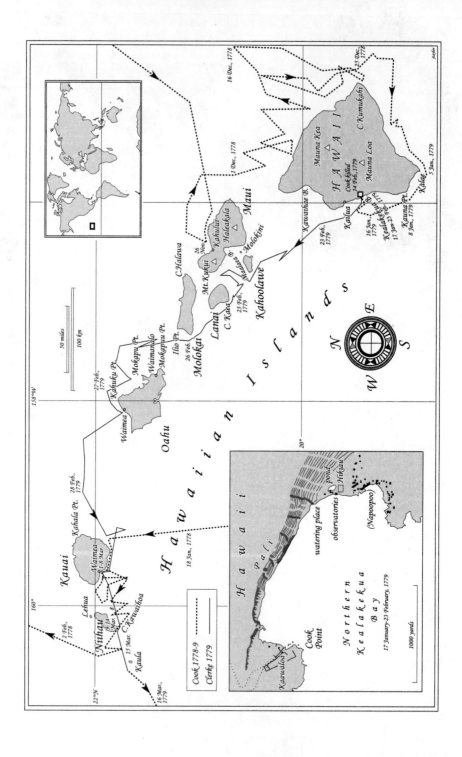

SEVEN

New Discoveries

The expedition set a course to the north. The Tahitians did not know of any islands in that direction and Cook did not expect to make a landfall until he encountered the west coast of North America. The *Discovery*, although she was the smaller ship, could sail faster than the *Resolution* — this was a complete contrast to Cook's previous voyage when the *Resolution* was always waiting for the *Adventure* to catch up with her. The arrangement was for the *Discovery* to press on ahead during the night and to wait for her consort to catch up in the morning. The winds were steady and progress was good. There was a great swell on the open sea and the winds blew fair. On the night of 22 December they crossed the equator and entered the northern hemisphere again. There were, of course, no duckings or celebrations, for every man had crossed the line at least once before but it was the first time one of Cook's ships had crossed the equator in the Pacific Ocean as opposed to the Atlantic. Two days later it was Christmas Eve and it came as a surprise when a small low island was seen to the north east. The island was protected by a coral reef and breaking over it was a high surf. It looked at first as though it would not be possible to make a landing but then a gap appeared through which the ships were able to sail. They named the place Christmas Island.

It was exactly a year since they had spent Christmas at Kerguelen

Island. Both islands were uninhabited but here was a very different terrain. There were no rocky cliffs or snow peaked mountains, but there were plenty of turtles and these provided sport and provisions. The sea was full of fish and there were many sharks which swam around the ships and broke the fishing lines. The land supported bushes and a few coconut trees, the only native fauna seemed to be rats and a small land bird, but there were many sea birds. The island was only three miles wide but it was over 20 miles in length, long enough for two of the turtle hunters to get themselves lost. The two were found the next day in a terrible state of exposure, for they were unable to find any fresh water. Cook stayed on a few days to observe an eclipse of the sun. These events figure very frequently in the log and in fact what he described as an eclipse was only a partial eclipse, but the observation was still useful for checking the longitude and the accuracy of the ship's chronometer. Cook left behind a bottle containing a message to claim his discovery of Christmas Island. The island was just capable of supporting man, in fact it had supported a resident human population in the past, but it was small and isolated and it was unlikely that any country would ever want to claim it for settlement.

The ships were soon off to the north again. Three uneventful weeks followed, but as they approached the tropic of Cancer there came a major surprise. At daylight on 18 January there was land to the north-east. It was a very different island from the one they had just left. It stood high out of the sea. This was an historic moment:

> At daylight this morning we discovered high land bearing NEbE for which we stood all day... We drew near the Land which we found to be a large Island, this appearing to us to be a new Discovery excited our Curiosity very much, expecting to meet with a new Race of People, distinct from the Islanders to the Southward of the Line; we were sometime in Suspense whether it was inhabited or not, however on approaching near to the SE end of the Island our doubts were cleared [by the] appearance of several canoes paddling towards us...[1]

As soon as the inhabitants reached the ship Cook offered them red cloth and nails, both of which were accepted with great pleasure. As they gathered around they shouted to each other and the British found that they could understand some of the words. Their language was very similar to that spoken at Tahiti. It was soon established that the produce of the island included hogs and fowl, breadfruit, sweet potatoes, sugar cane and cocoa. It was a great bonus to be able to get fresh supplies before they reached the coast of America. By this time there were several islands in view and it became obvious they had stumbled across a new island group. The islands were green and fertile and this time, unlike Christmas Island, they were inhabited. The British did not know the extent of the archipelago. The crews of the *Resolution* and *Discovery* were the first Europeans to gaze on the exotic islands of Hawaii. They did not yet know that they had made a major discovery. Was it luck or was it genius? Genius generates its own luck. Captain Cook had still not lost his touch.

The 'big island' of Hawaii lay to the east and it was below the horizon; they had stumbled across the smaller islands of Oahu, Kauai and Niihau. On 19 January they were offshore from Kauai when the crowd of excited islanders came out in their canoes to welcome them. The visit generated excitement on both sides. The Hawaiians had never experienced contact with the outside world before. As a race they were similar in appearance to the Tahitians but they were darker skinned. As the chattering natives swarmed around the ship the British thought they could recognise some of the words. Soon there was no doubt that they spoke a language very similar to Tahitian. How Cook must have wished that he still had Omai on board to assist with the communications problems.

There were 40° of latitude between Tahiti and Hawaii, nearly 2,500 miles of ocean. If these people spoke Tahitian then how did they come to be here? There was no written history of a great sea saga to support the tradition that they had crossed so much of the Pacific. There was the one stepping stone at Christmas Island. They had canoes which could travel around their own local group of islands. But how did they cross the vast ocean? How did they navigate? How did they know the islands were there in the first place? If they came from Tahiti, or wherever they had come from, then how did they cross the ocean in numbers great enough to create a settled population without the problem of incest? Cook had met the conundrum several times before. He found a similar situation on his first landing in New Zealand when the Maori language was found to have similarities to Tahitian. He had also seen it in the Marquesas. He had experienced it on Easter Island, a spot which was even more isolated than Hawaii. There was one clue to the mystery, which he had in fact witnessed on this very voyage. He remembered the Tahitians who had accidentally found themselves carried to the Tonga Islands. There was proof that large distances could be covered by the Polynesian canoes. It was the navigation problems and the migration in sufficient numbers which were difficult to explain.

Cook found it hard to believe that he was the first discoverer of Hawaii. The Spanish, after all, had been crossing the North Pacific for centuries but no sightings in these parts had ever been reported. Even Francis Drake, who sailed across the Pacific from San Francisco in the sixteenth century, could hardly have missed passing through the Hawaii archipelago but he too had not claimed the discovery. Cook looked for evidence of other ships which might have been there before him. There was iron, but only in very small quantities, and closer inquiry showed that it had been brought in on the tide as driftwood from an unknown far distant wreck on a far distant shore.

The assumption that the Polynesian race was indigenous to Tahiti was wrong in the first place. Even in Cook's time the most likely theory was that the Pacific Islands had been first inhabited from the west. The adventurers had moved from island to island, from group to group, by stages in a fantastic history from so long ago that it had not even survived in their oral traditions. The story had never been recorded, fragments of it remained in the folklore but once the migrations passed out of living memory the facts became very distorted. It is easy to conceive how islands 20 or even 50 miles away could be discovered by fishermen or by small groups of explorers. It is possible to see how their navigation was good enough for them to get home again and even to be able to take a fleet of canoes to colonise a new island. But in the case of Hawaii the Tahitian canoes had crossed thousands of miles of ocean. The migrations had taken place thousands of years ago, yet much of their language and culture remained the same. Perhaps it was all an accident. There had been expeditions between islands which had been blown way off course by storm and weather, accidentally finding a new island on which to set up home. For every successful such expedition how many had perished unknown in the great blue of the infinite Pacific? It was a story as moving and incredible as any on earth.

The first contact between the primitive Hawaiians and the British was described in the journal of Lieutenant James King of the *Resolution*. The Hawaiians were invited on board the ship. They were fascinated by the many strange materials that they had never seen before:

We took some of them into the Gunroom to observe their behavior & to put Questions to them; when we askd them what this Iron was, & where it came from. they told us, they did not know but that we knew; when we shewd them beads they askd if they shou'd eat them, or what was their use, we told them only to hang to their Ears, on which they returnd them to us as useless, for their ears are not pierced; they also returnd looking Glasses, saying they did not know what these things were for; & of Iron they only knew its use for boring & to make Toes (Hatchets) & wantd them large, they observd with attention our Cloaths, & seem'd to think the Substance different from their own; but at first they took Otaheite Cloth to be the same, however they soon tried if it wou'd tear, which finding it to do,they did not care for it; they were quite Ignorant of what our China cups were made of, taking them for wood, asking for some, that those on shore might look at them. They were very curious & doubtful what our Ships Sails &c were made of. In their behaviour they were very fearful of giving offence, asking if they should sit down, or spit on the decks &c, & in all their conduct seemd to regard us as superior beings.[2]

The scene on board the *Discovery* was very similar and is described by the captain, Charles Clerke. A minor accident, when a cabin window slammed shut, sent the boarders scampering off in terror through the port holes:

> My Cabin was at one time full of them, but was soon clear'd by the following Accident; my Guests were exceedingly curious and very desirous of handling and examining whatever came in their way, especially if composed of their favourite Metal, Iron; the Cabin Windows were open and suspended by Iron Hooks; one of them in examining one of these Hooks, withdrew its support from the window, which immediately shut down like a Trap Door; something of the kind I believe my poor friends took it for, for they directly made their way out at the other windows (some of which by their crouding they broke in their way) with as much confusion and fright, as tho' a battery had been opened upon them; we were going upwards of 4 knots at the time, however their canoes picked them up. —[3]

At the island of Kauai John Williamson was sent to get water. It was hardly surprising that a great crowd of Hawaiians flocked around in excitement and wanted to help to fill the casks. The watering party was accompanied by a detachment of marines with muskets but of course the local people had no idea that the muskets could kill them. Williamson estimated the reception committee to be over a hundred, they were so numerous that he tried to retreat and find another place where it was less crowded. The crowd clung onto the boat and would not allow it to go out again.

The Hawaiins were scrambling into the boat in such numbers that the boat heeled over and was in danger of overturning. One Hawaiian tried to steal the boat hook. Williamson tried to force him off and offered him a nail instead. The man would not give way, he was determined to have the boat hook and in desperation Williamson shot him.

The man dropped dead in the water and his blood came to the surface. When they saw the power of the musket the Hawaiians retreated, but when the British too had left the scene they returned to collect the body. Williamson claimed that all his men wanted to shoot at the Hawaiians, but he ordered them to hold their fire.

Williamson fired the only shot. The watering was completed and he decided not to tell Captain Cook about the incident, a serious error of judgement on his part. Gossip about the power of the musket was all over the island, it would get to the ears of the captain very quickly and the men in the watering party would soon be telling their accounts of the shooting to their shipmates. Cook did not discover about the shooting however, until after they had left the islands. There was one good thing which came out of the incident. The fact that the Hawaiians knew about the potency of the firearms made life easier for the landing parties and ensured more respect when the marines appeared armed with their muskets.

The ubiquitous pilfering problem was as bad, if not worse than anywhere else in the Pacific, but the trade was excellent, and the natives were so eager to have objects made of metal that a day's supply of pork could be obtained for a single spike nail. The ship's blacksmith hammered the nails into primitive chisels and these were considered by the islanders to be of even greater value than the nails. This first contact showed that there were many similarities, besides the common language, between the Hawaiians and the other Polynesian peoples. Some of the women were very eager to give their sexual favours but this time Cook completely forbade his men to have any sexual contact. He knew that the ships carried venereal disease with them. Thomas Edgar, master of the *Discovery*, described the situation in his journal when the women begged to be allowed on board the ship:

> None of them were permitted to come on board the Ships & every precaution was taken to prevent the Men from medling with them on Shore & this requir'd the utmost vigilance of the Officers for the Women us'd all their Arts to entice them into their Houses, & even

went so far as to Endeavour to draw them in by force And tho none who
we re known to have that dreadful distemper upon them we re suffe red
to set their foot on Shore, nor even those who had been but lately out
of the Surgeon's List Yet the great eagerness of the Women concurring
with the Desires of the Men it became impossible to keep them from
each other & we had reason to beleive that some of them had
Connections with these Woman both on board our Ships & on Shore,
Notwithstanding every precaution that was taken to Prevent it.[4]

The Hawaiian girls were not to be put off so easily. Some of them
disguised themselves as men to gain access to the ships. William
Bradley was given a dozen lashes for taking one of the women, the
punishment was severe because he had been diagnosed with venereal
disease and Cook wanted to make an example out of him.

On the next day the weather took a turn for the worse. It was
typical of the weather in this part of the Pacific in that it changed very
quickly. A sudden storm blew up and Cook did not feel safe with his
anchorage on a lee shore. He gave orders to sail further out from the
land but as they got underway Samuel Gibson, a veteran marine of all
three of Cook's voyages, was the worse for drink and he fell overboard.
A new machine, invented for precisely this eventuality, was brought
into action and thrown into the water. It was a wooden frame kept
afloat by cork and it carried a bell to sound the whereabouts of the man
overboard. The machine did in fact serve its purpose, but not very effi-
ciently for Gibson found it impossible to keep the contraption upright
when he was sitting on the cork seat. The bad weather had carried the
Resolution near to the neighbouring island of Niihau and Cook decided
to make a landing there. It had a good water supply and he decided to
leave goats, pigs and seeds with a person who seemed to have some
authority there.

The journals recorded many details about the life and customs on
Hawaii on this the very first contact with Europe. Some of the women
wore feather ruffs around their necks, made of red, yellow and black
feathers. They had bracelets made from turtle shell and necklaces of

small shells and large boars' teeth. James King noted that at Tahiti it was common to find women with their ears bored for ear rings but this was not the case at Hawaii. Both peoples wore necklaces. There was much in common with the mode of dress, adding to the evidence that the races had a common origin. The feathered cloaks and head-dresses were only worn on special occasions, they set great value by them and they were unwilling to trade them. The head-dresses were woven in basket work and covered with short red feathers, then streaks of yellow, black and green feathers were intermixed. They were made to fit close to the head, with small semicircular spaces left for the ears. In the middle of the cap was built a ridge or protuberance about 3 inches high and about the same in width, it extended along the whole length of the cap, the upper part forming a larger curve at the front, shaped like the bill of a bird. The ridge was often covered with long red feathers and gave the cap a strong resemblance to a classical ancient helmet.

The cloaks were made of netting with feathers of various colours worked into the mesh of the net. They came in different lengths and they were fashioned to be considerably wider at the bottom than at the top. Cook's men thought they resembled the short Spanish cloaks often seen in prints of the time. The most valuable of these cloaks were made of red and yellow feathers, artistically arranged to have a fine effect and a very striking appearance. There were lesser cloaks fashioned from the feathers of sea birds, but these were of far less value. James King wondered about the similarities between artefacts and religion in Hawaii and Tahiti:

There doubtless cannot be a subject more liable to error than in deducing the origin of a people from certain resemblances in their religious ceremonies, their arts & their manners; & in drawing conclusions from such similarity amongst the different Islands in these seas, would be very fallacious; for as they are nearly in the same state of Civilisation, & as their Climates & country have so much resemblance, the effects of the former will be nearly equal in all, & the same wants in the latter will produce like efforts, from which a great similitude will arise in their Arts & manners; & as to religious ceremonies, what with the difficulty of the subject & from the superstitious rights of uninformed nations being built on a principal of fear to invisible beings, there will be often a great likeness in their ceremonies. Although no solid inferences can be found from such conclusions, yet they may be brought in addition or at least not as contradicting an opinion founded on better grounds.[5]

Cook could now trace the extent of the Polynesian people simply from the places where the language was spoken. He had been to New Zealand, the Tonga Isles, Tahiti and now Hawaii. On his previous voyages he had visited the isolated Easter Island and the Marquesas. At all these locations he had gathered as many words as he could of the native language. It was possible for the anthropologists to identify different dialects on the different island groups but it was obvious that the same language was spoken in all places. What was not so obvious was where the race originated and what was the direction in which they travelled and populated the Pacific. King argued that although the Polynesians were not as numerous as other nations, their country was spread over an area comparable to the great continents of Africa and Asia:

> The Knowledge of this wide extensive nation, their Manners, their Arts & of the different Islands they inhabit, add a lustre on our nation, & gives it a decided advantage over all others, in her Naval skill & in the Spirit of their enterprises; & which every good subject must rejoice to see; & hope, that no event will ever happen to abate or confine the influence of such a spirit.[6]

It was a marvellous bonus for the voyage to have discovered the Hawaiian Islands. Cook would have loved to have stayed longer to map and chart them more thoroughly, it was annoying that so much time had been spent on previously discovered islands when there was such an exciting new find to be explored. The situation had suddenly changed from one where there was time to kill to one where time was at a premium. There simply was not enough time to stay and search for more islands. The season was moving on and there was still a lot of exploration before them if they were to find the North West Passage. Cook here showed great loyalty but a singular lack of imagination by naming the Hawaiian islands after the first lord of the admiralty, Lord Sandwich. This was a name he had already used for other groups of islands, notably in the South Atlantic. It was a name which fortunately hardly anybody took any notice of. The islands reverted to the native name of Hawaii, used by those who came after him.

At this his first visit Cook saw only five Hawaiian islands and he landed on only two of them. He knew from the native people that there existed more islands to the south east. He knew that he had stumbled upon an important new archipelago with supplies of wood, food and water. He knew that there was a great anthropological question to be studied. Yet, where at Tahiti he had had time to spare, he was now short of time for he had to be in the far north as soon as the season would allow him to take advantage of the receding ice in the northern latitudes. Only two islands had been explored, only three had been put on the chart. On 2 February he sailed for America. It was not his custom to discuss his plans with his senior officers but he knew in his mind that he could return to these islands for supplies after the search for the North West Passage. Did this decision not to chart the whole Hawaiian archipelago imply that he had lost confidence in finding a route to the Atlantic?

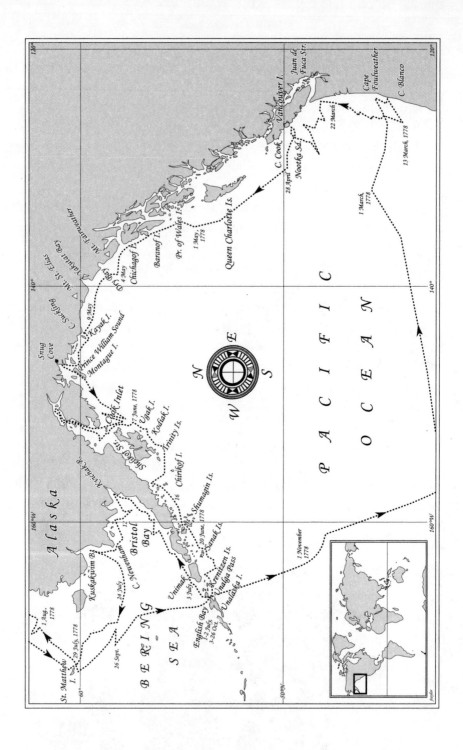

EIGHT

America Unknown

The crossing of the Pacific from Hawaii to the coast of America took five uneventful weeks sailing across an empty ocean. On the first day of March the convoy's latitude was measured at 44° 49'. Seals and whales had appeared in the seas and on 6 March the Pacific coastline of America was sighted at a latitude of about 45°. The English called the place New Albion in memory of Drake's famous voyage around the world in 1579, almost two centuries before Cook. Francis Drake, having plundered the Spanish Main to his heart's content, had sailed up the western coast of North America carrying so much silver and gold that he could discard much of his ballast. He sailed as far as Drake's Bay just north of San Francisco. The extent of Drake's voyage, and how far north he explored, is still the subject of some controversy. At one point Drake considered searching for a North West Passage and he may well have got as far as the 49th parallel but his records are not detailed enough to prove the point. Cook, on his approach to America, was blown south to a latitude of 42° 45' where he may just have been able to see the northernmost part of California. The two Englishmen, separated by two hundred years, may well have navigated along part of the same coastline.

The first impression of the American coastline was formidable. The foothills of the Rocky Mountains towered above, their snow-covered peaks so high they were often hidden in the clouds. Great flocks of birds flew shrieking above the ship and landed in the rigging. The tropical climate was far behind and the weather was fog, hail, sleet and snow. The virgin forest was populated by great trees, American pine, spruce and redwood, some of which had been growing for a thousand years and a few which had been saplings at the birth of Christ. They lined the coast right down to the water line. The fine timber was exactly what Cook needed. Cook's first priority was to repair his ships. The masts, spars and rigging were all in a very poor state and they were not sound enough to face a season of exploration in the icy seas of the far north. He searched to find a place where his split mast could be replaced and where the ships could be repaired and overhauled for their coming ordeal. It was not easy to find a sheltered harbour with such a formidable coastline and it took him three weeks to find a suitable cove.

It is difficult to pass by places on the coast of America without reference to the modern place names, none of which were finalised in 1778 at the latitudes where the *Resolution* and the *Discovery* were busy mapping and charting. The country was well populated, the Indians had many place names and Cook put these on his charts on the rare occasions when he was able to discover them. The cove, which Cook thought lay on the American mainland, was in fact on the coast of a very long island. If Cook had possessed a crystal ball to gaze into the future he would have been surprised and pleased to find that the densely wooded coast where he anchored would be named by posterity after one of his own men. That man was George Vancouver, a midshipman on the *Discovery* who had sailed on Cook's second voyage with the *Resolution*, and who came back in the 1790s to survey the Canadian coastline. Vancouver was honoured for his work not only with a great island but a great city being named after him as well.

It was a very difficult coast for a sailing vessel. The prevailing winds were continually carrying the ship onto the formidable rocks. The wind was cold but the month was still February and the sun's warmth could not therefore be expected at this time of the year. When he managed to strike up trade with the Indians Cook discovered that the local name of the inlet was pronounced 'Nootka' and he therefore named the place Nootka Sound. Both his ships were in a very poor state of repair, the *Resolution*'s timbers were rotten, the rats were steadily gnawing their way into the stores and the cockroaches had multiplied to plague proportions. The deterioration left a great question mark over the refurbishing at the Deptford yard, for it seems that many of the main timbers had not been replaced and even where they had the replacements were of such poor quality that they had lasted for less than two years at sea. The first priority was to make the ships seaworthy for the formidable task which lay ahead but at least British Columbia was very well supplied with some of the world's finest timber. Cook described the fitting of the new fore mast and he tells of some of the botched workmanship:

In the afternoon we resumed our work and the next day rigged the Foremast; the head of which being rather too small for the Cap, the Carpenter went to work to bring or fix a piece on one side to fill up the Gap. In cutting into the mast head for this purpose, and examining a little farther into it, both cheeks were found so rotton that there was no possibility of repairing them without geting the mast out and fixing on new ones. It was evedent that one of the Cheeks had been defective at the first, and the defective part had been cut out and a piece put [in], what had not only weakened the mast head, but had in a great measure been the occasion of roting all the other part. Thus when we were almost ready to put to Sea, we had all our work to do over again, and what was worse a job of work to perform that required some time to finish but there was no remedy we immediately set about it. It was lucky the defects were descovered in a place where wood, the principal thing wanting was to be had; for among the drift wood in the Cove where we lay, were some well seasoned trees and very proper for our purpose, one of which was pitched upon and the Carpenters went to work to make out of it two new Cheeks.[1]

Cook's account describes the fore mast, but the mizzen mast also needed replacing and work on it was started the next day. The American Indians were full of curiosity and they arrived in their canoes, willing enough to trade fish and vegetables. About thirty canoes had appeared and the Indians began to gain confidence — they were soon shouting loudly and pointing. After a time they began to sing, in a very wild manner, in their own language of which not a single word was understood. King tells of one man with a soft effeminate voice who sang a solo and beat the sides of his canoe in time with the rhythm. The other Indians joined in a chorus. Then the soloist ended his song suddenly and unexpectedly but with such a peculiar gesture that the British laughed out loud. Pleased with the reaction he repeated the song and the gesture several times. Then the British, not to be outdone, brought out the fife and drum and they even produced two French horns. The Americans listed in attentive silence.

The musical interlude was a good prelude to trade. The metal items which the British used for barter were not valued as highly in America as they were on Hawaii and the reason was that the Indians already had plenty of metal objects. The Spanish, who had made settlements to the south, did not venture as far north as Oregon to trade, but their items had been exchanged by the Indian tribes all along the coast and they had reached to the high latitudes of British Columbia. A good example was a pair of silver spoons which were spotted hanging around the neck of one of the Indians, who willingly exchanged the spoons for a pewter hand washing bowl. He obviously knew nothing of the value of silver.

Whilst the ships were refitting Cook was able to explore the coast-line using the ships' boats. Some of his expeditions were very long, up to 30 miles of rowing, and Cook decided that the young midshipmen were the ideal workhorses for the task. The Cornishman Trevenen described one such outing. His description is a very valuable passage for it shows that on at least one occasion the severe and unapproach-able Captain Cook actually relaxed his authority to 'converse famil-iarly' with the midshipmen. It lasted but a very short time and the magic soon disappeared when Cook returned to his ship:

> We were fond of such excursions, altho' the labour of them was very
> great, as, not only this kind of duty, was more agreeable than the
> humdrum routine on board the ships, but as it gave us an opportunity
> of viewing the different people & countries, and as another very prin-
> cipal consideration we were sure of having plenty to eat & drink,
> which was not always the case on board the Ship on our usual
> allowance. Capt. Cooke also on these occasions, would sometimes relax
> from his almost constant severity of disposition, & condescend now
> and then, to converse familiarly with us But it was only for the time,
> as soon as we entered the ships, he became again the despot.[2]

The many months in the Pacific Islands had given the men a taste for
local girls. The Indian girls did not offer their services as readily as the
maidens of the warmer climates. Their attraction was not enhanced by
the fact that they washed very seldom, if at all and they were very
dirty. To make matters worse it was the height of fashion to cover
themselves in a revolting red ochre which had to be washed off before
they were in any way presentable. Samwell described the cleansing
process:

> Hitherto we had seen none of their young Women tho' we had often
> given the men to understand how agreeable their Company would be
> to us & how profitable to themselves, in consequence of which they
> about this time brought two or three Girls to the Ships; tho' some of
> them had no bad faces yet as they were exceedingly dirty their Persons
> at first sight were not very inviting, however our young Gentlemen
> were not to be discouraged by such an obstacle as this which they
> found was to be removed with Soap & warm water, this they called the
> Ceremony of Purification and were themselves the Officiators at it, &
> it must be mentioned to their praise that they performed it with much
> piety & Devotion, taking as much pleasure in cleansing a naked young
> Woman from all Impurities in a Tub of Warm Water, as a young

Confessor would to absolve a beautiful Virgin who was about to sacrifice that Name to himself. This Ceremony appeared very strange to the Girls, who in order to render themselves agreeable to us had taken particular pains to daub their Hair and faces well with red oaker which to their great astonishment we took as much pains to wash off. Such are the different Ideas formed by different nations of Beauty & cleanliness; they were prevailed upon to sleep on board the Ships, or rather forced to it by their Fathers or other Relations who brought them on board. In their behaviour they were very modest and timid, in which they differed very much from the South Sea Island Girls who in general are impudent & loud.[3]

On 21 April the ships were ready to continue their journey northwards along the coast. As the ships worked their way out of Nootka Sound the winds were changeable and progress was very slow. As they got underway in these weather conditions Cook was obliged to stand well off from such a dangerous coastline and consequently his charting of the land was far from complete. It could hardly have been a more difficult coastline to chart. Even when the visibility was good it was impossible to tell islands from promontries. The coast broke into myriad islands which would take months or even years to map and chart. Cook's instructions from his superiors were very clear, he was not to explore all the inlets and rivers, time did not allow it. He continued to explore northwards as best he could and by the end of April the ships had reached a latitude of 53°. It was here that the crude map of Admiral de Fonte showed a fictional strait cutting right across the American continent. There was indeed a passage of some kind but it was obvious from the backdrop of the great mountains that it was no more than a river estuary.

The expedition sailed on. Soon it was obvious that they were being forced to the west by the coastline. There was no passage to the north. They passed the Yukon territory and entered the forbidding coast of Alaska. The snows were now no longer confined to the higher slopes of the mountains, the snowfields reached right down to the shoreline.

Other ships had perished on this dangerous coast and Cook knew that hereabouts the Russian explorer Vitus Bering had lost a ship and a whole crew about thirty-seven years ago. Some of Cook's crew had fanciful ideas about finding shipwrecked Russian sailors, ancient and bearded, still surviving in the wilds. We cannot leave the area without a further mention of George Vancouver, and a quote from Vancouver's own account of the coastline which he wrote a decade later. Vancouver describes what Cook called Bering Bay and he proved that it was not a bay at all:

The part of the coast off which we had been thus cruising since the preceding thursday, appeared from its latitude, and relative situation with these two very conspicuous mountains [St Elias and Fairweather] to be that part where Captain Cook supposed that Beering had anchored, and to which he gave the name of Beering, supposing it to be a bay, with an island covered with wood lying off its southern part. But in this neighbourhood no such bay or island exists, and Captain Cook must have been led into the mistake by the great distance at which he saw this coast; in consequence of which he was prevented noticing the extensive border of low land that stretches from the foot of the vast range of lofty mountains, and forms the sea shore. The irregularity of the base of these mountains, which retire in some places to a considerable distance, and especially in the part now alluded to, would, on a more remote view than we had taken, lead the most cautious observer to consider the appearances in the coast, as indicating deep bays, or openings likely to afford tolerable, and even good shelter; and had it not been from the information we had previously received from Mr. Brown, who had been close in with these shores, we should have still supposed, until thus far advanced, that we had Beering's bay in view, with the island lying near its south-eastern point. This deception is occasioned by a ramification of the mountains stretching towards the ocean, and terminating in a perpendicular cliff, as if at the sea side; having a more elevated part of the low border, covered with wood, lying to the south-west of it; the former at a

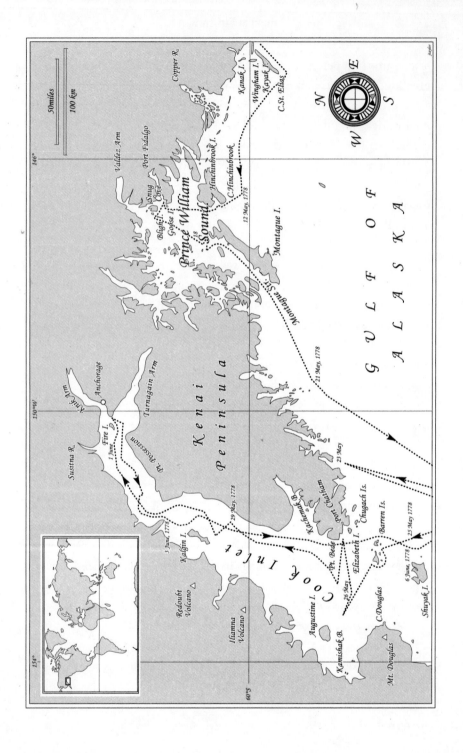

distance, appears to form the east point of an extensive bay, and the
latter, an island lying off from it; but both these are at the distance of
some miles from the sea shore, which from port Mulgrave [in Yakutat
Bay] to this station takes a general direction about S, 65 E. and is
chiefly composed of a very low tract of land, terminating in sandy
beaches...[4]

The *Resolution* had sprung a leak in her buttocks — this was the name
given to the stern of the ship adjacent to the rudder. The leak was just
above the water line but on the starboard tack the roll of the ship
caused water to flow into the bread store. The leak was bad news
coming so soon after the overhaul for the new masts. A harbour was
needed to stop and repair the leak. Cook found a bay which he called
Snug Cove where the leak was repaired after a fashion, but it was only
a botched job for what the ship really needed was to be taken apart and
the rotted timbers replaced. There was no oakum at all left in the crack
and the hole was so wide that a one and a half inch hawser was needed
to plug it. Inquisitive Indians appeared and nosed around the ships
during the stay at Snug Cove. They were even uglier than the Indians
to the south. They believed in mutilating their faces in a horrible and
disgusting fashion. The first time they were seen a rumour spread
around the ships that they were a race of people with two mouths:

Some both men and women have the under lip slit quite through hori-
zontally and so large as to admit the tongue which I have seen them
thrust through, which happened to be the case when it was first
discovered by one of the Seamen, who called out there was a man with
two mouths and indeed it does not look unlike it. Though the lips of
all were not slit, yet all were bored, espicially the women and even the
young girls; to these holes and slits they fix pieces of bone of this size
([a blank space]) and shape, placed side by side in the inside of the
lip; a thread is run through them to keep them together, and some goes
quite through the lip and fastens, or fore-locks' on the out side to
which they hang other pieces of bones or beads. This Ornament is a

very great impediment to the Speach and makes them look as if they
had a double row of teeth in the under jaw. Besides these lip jewels
which they seemed to value above all others, they wear a bone, or some
bugle beads strung on a stif string or Cord 3 or 4 inch long, run
through the cartilage that divides the nostrils from each other. Their
ears are bored all round to which they hang beads or pieces of bone;
they wear braclets and some other ornaments and to crown all they
use both black and red paint so that I have nowhere seen Indians that
take more pains to ornament, or rather disfigure themselves, than
these people.[5]

The Indians were not co-operative. At Snug Cove the *Resolution* was
heeled over to larboard so that the leak could be repaired. This
brought the lower hatches, called the scuttles, very close to the water
line. The scuttles were lined with glass behind the hatches. The
Indians took the opportunity to reach the glass from their canoes, they
broke every one of the scuttle glasses and took the broken glass to
trade amongst themselves. There were only three sailors on the deck of
the ship and the Indians calculated that they could easily overpower
them. They started by stealing everything moveable from the decks.
When they realised what was happening the British called down to
those below decks for assistance, and their shipmates came rushing
onto the deck brandishing their cutlasses. Luckily, this show of force
was sufficient to frighten off the Indians, they fled from the ship and,
by motioning with their arms, they indicated to their colleagues the
great length of the knives with which the defenders were armed.

After leaving Snug Cove the lie of the land continued to prevent any
progress to the north. The two ships had to sail west again in the hope
of finding a way around to the north and west. They arrived at an inlet
which seemed large enough to be a sea passage. There was an expanse
of water as far as the eye could see. Was it a passage through the
American continent? Cook thought it was worthwhile exploring and
for a few days it seemed as though there could be a sea passage through
Alaska to the north. By 1 June however, the ships had gone far enough

(Previous Page) Portrait of Captain James Cook 1776, by John Webber. The artist's portrait shows James Cook, in full dress uniform with sword and telescope on his third voyage. He looks younger than his forty-eight years but the artist shows a facial expression of thought and determination in keeping with Cook's character.

(Left) *The Resolution*, pencil drawing by John Webber. The sketch was made to help the artist with the more detailed pictures of the ships that he painted later in the voyage. There are no figures to give a sense of scale, but the overall impression is accurate and impressive.

View of Adventure Bay, Van Diemans Lan

Cook's Reception at Ha'apai, Tonga by John Webber. The artist gives a very vivid impression of the contact between two cultures. The excitement and the grand scale of the reception are obvious. The Tongans are shown climbing the trees to obtain a better view of what appears to be a club dance.

(Left) *View of Adventure Bay, Van Dieman's Land* by William Ellis. The artist gives a simple view of the bay named after the ship *Adventure* on Cook's second voyage. It is a valuable contribution to the history of Tasmania, very few ships had made a landing there before Cook's voyages.

A Human Sacrifice in Tahiti by John Webber. Tahitian society had much to admire in it, but human ㅤ rifice was known to be practised on occasions such as when prisoners of war were taken. Here th ㅤ drums are beating and preparations for the sacrifice are well underway. The third figure on the r ㅤ appears to be Captain Cook.

Tahitian Dancing by John Webber. All the Polynesian cultures had music, song and dance. Webber's picture shows the musicians with drums, the women in elaborate costumes and both sexes executing specific dance motions on a specially prepared floor.

The Anchorage at Nootka Sound by John Webber. Nootka Sound was Cook's first anchorage on the north-west coast of America. It was the place where timber was felled to repair the ships for their journey to the north. Webber shows plenty of action, many boats and trade with the Indians.

King William Sound by John Webber. This shows the grandeur of the mountain scenery of Alaska the expedition worked its way towards the west and the north the ships were dwarfed by the wo nature.

Meeting with the Chukchi at St Lawrence Bay by John Webber. The Chukchi survived in the icy eastern regions of Siberia by hunting and fishing. Cook's party is shown seated. The meeting is a good example of Cook's first contact with unknown peoples.

(Right) Captain Charles Clerke by Nathaniel Dance. Charles Clerke sailed on all three of Cook's great voyages. After Cook's death at Kealakekua Bay he took command of the expedition, but he was very ill and he only lived for a few more months. Clerke was a fine man who did his duty right to the end of his life.

(Left) *Kealakekua Bay with the ships at anchor* by William Ellis. The artist shows the *Resolution* and *Discovery* at anchor in Kealakekua Bay. The detail shows the trees and shrubs along the shoreline, the mountains behind the bay and double hulled Hawaiian canoes complete with sails.

Death of Captain Cook at Kealakekua Bay 14 February 1779 by John Cleveley. Cleveley's painting sh⟨ows⟩
the scene in Kealakekua Bay as Captain Cook fights desperately for his life. The ship's boats are ⟨in⟩
support, but in the confusion they are not near enough to give help. The scene was reconstructe⟨d⟩
from the account and sketches made by James Cleveley, a carpenter on board the *Resolution*, and ⟨the⟩
picture was painted at a later date by his brother John.

This detail shows C⟨ook⟩
wielding his musket ⟨to⟩
fend off his attacker⟨s.⟩
The account conflic⟨ts⟩
with other descripti⟨ons⟩
of Cook's death, bu⟨t it⟩
must be accepted th⟨at⟩
the incident depicte⟨d⟩
here was the view o⟨f an⟩
eye witness.

into the inlet to find that it was reduced to no more than a river estuary. Before turning to the south again Cook decided to make a claim to the country. James King recorded the incident in his journal:

> As all prospects of finding a passage to an open sea by this Inlet is now given over, & which I believe every one is satisfy'd to be only the Entrance of a large & possibly a very extensive river, the Captn before his return out of it sent me to the North point of the Eastern low land, there to take Possesion of all the Country, in the Name & for the use of his Majesty & his Successors. In our way thither we calld on board the *Discovery* & took their Cutter with us, in which was Mr Bailey & the Doctor. As we came near the Shore, we saw about a dozen of the Natives on the top of the rising ground, extending their Arms & inviting us on shore; they however appeard in much agitation, which put us on our Guard; when we landed there were about a Dozn on the beach ...
>
> After some time we returnd to our Party & performd the Ceremony of taking Possession, by hoisting Colours &c; & drinking his Majestys health in good English Porter, by us, as well as by three of the Natives who repeated what we said; (& what we did not expect) were fond of the Liquor; they had also the empty Bottles; we contriv'd to place a bottle that the Captn had given us (with a Parchment Scroll in it) not in a conspicuous open place, for that the Natives would find, but under some rocks by the Side of a Stuntd tree, where if it escapes the Indians, in many ages hence it may Puzle Antiquarians.[6]

It took two weeks to explore the inlet but there was obviously no way through the continent. The land, which had been running to the west, now actually seemed to turn to the south, the wrong direction altogether. It was all very frustrating. Two more of the sails had split and many others looked about to follow suit. The expedition struggled on and the coastline forced them to sail further and further to the south. On the longest day, 21 June, at a latitude of 54° 27', they encountered a great volcano sending vapours up to the sky as high as the eye could see. The waters around these parts were treacherous with hidden currents, there was fog and the winds blew from variable directions. At one point a passage was discovered between the mainland and an island. The rush of water suggested that it was a passage to the other side of a promontory. The *Resolution* got through the passage safely but the *Discovery* was caught by a change in the tide and she found herself floundering in a small whirlpool. It was a close call:

> Weighed and made sail to the NW through between two islands — but at 7 the ebb tide met us from the north — running so strong that we could not stem it tho we had a fine breeze at SSW . The tide runs near 6 Knots. Which makes a very great Race, & rough Sea breaking in on the Ships decks. It carried our Ship round & round several times & was near carrying us on some broken rocks that lay of the point of an Island — but however we drove clear of all out into a more open part where it left us...[7]

There was one piece of good fortune when the seine netted a fine catch of cod, but this was offset by a fog so thick that it was not possible to see one end of the ship from the other. The fog was so dense that the top gallants were out of sight. The ships had been sailing the length of the treacherous Alaskan Peninsula. But at last it was apparent that the land was breaking up into a string of islands. This was the archipelago of the Aleutians and the string of islands was 1,000 miles long. Cook remained unaware of the archipelago, as even if he had had good visibility the islands reached far out of sight into the North Pacific. They had found the passage now known as the Unalga Pass between the islands of Unalaska and Krenitzen. There was still thick fog but the tide was right and the wind was favourable. They had been forced to travel south down to a latitude of less than 54° but when they had navigated through the pass the way was clear at last to head to the north again.

On one of the foraging expeditions one of the seaman met with an Indian who gave him a box with a wooden whistle inside. He tried to blow it but with no success. Then he opened it up to find a note written in a language he did not understand. The language was Russian. What the explorers did not know was that the Russian trading post was only a few miles away, on the same island of Unalaska.

There was a small cove where the ships stopped for a few days. Captain Cook went grouse shooting with some of his officers. Canoes came round to trade and John Gore went with David Samwell and others to visit an Indian village with the strange name of Samganooda which was only a short distance away. The village lay in a low valley and as they approached there was a great quantity of fish hanging out to dry. At first there appeared to be no dwelling houses but then some small hillocks were discovered each with a hole in the top. The hillocks were the entrances to the underground dwellings. They were invited to go inside, access was down a wooden ladder into what seemed like a dark and dirty cave about 10 yards long and 5 in width. There was a stink of fish and worse, there was a large bowl of stale urine and human faeces. At one end was a fireplace for heating and cooking and with smaller rooms also sunk into the earth. There was a loft where seal skins were stored, whale gut and other commodities. The only light seemed to come from the roof where they had entered. The visit lasted about two hours and during this time John Webber made sketches from which he was able to draw his pictures. They found that the Indians had supplies of tobacco which they knew could not have been grown locally. Other objects of trade appeared which were not made by the Indians but neither had they come from the Spanish trade to the south. The clues to the trading patterns were there, the Indians were trading with the Russians who had crossed the Bering Sea from their settlements in Siberia.

It was July and Cook was anxious to be on his way again. It had taken months to navigate the American coast, the summer months were already upon them and they seemed to have made no progress at all towards the North West Passage. They followed the coastline on the north side of the Alaskan Peninsula and they came to another promising inlet. As with the Cook Inlet it had to be investigated. It transpired that it was not even a river estuary, it was merely a deep bay with no passage through the continent. Cook named it Bristol Bay after the Earl of Bristol, it was a big bay but another disappointment and it cost him three weeks of valuable searching time. The wind changed to the south west and the ships made out to sea again. Cook spent hours and hours frowning and puzzling over his maps. He was desperately trying to identify the islands shown on the maps of Stahlin, Muller and Bering. He had yet to discover that the maps were very misleading, all three were so inaccurate that they were more of a hindrance to him than a help. On the few occasions when the sun became visible the latitude was found to be approaching 60° once more. The little convoy sailed on with the natural silence broken by the sound of drums, bells and guns so that the two ships did not lose each other in the fog.

Then, on the first day of August, came a very sad blow. William Anderson, the ship's surgeon, finally succumbed to consumption. His death was a terrible loss, he was a man who had been an inspiration on the voyage. Not only did the expedition lose its leading medical practitioner but also it weakened the scientific contribution, for Anderson was well versed in botany and zoology, more so than anybody else on the expedition:

> Mr Anderson my Surgeon who had been lingering under a consumption for more than twelve Months, expired between 3 and 4 this after noon. He was a Sensible Young Man, an agreeable companion, well skilld in his profession, and had acquired much knowlidge in other Sciences that had it pleased God to have spar'd his life might have been useful in the Course of the Voyage.[8]

Cook wanted to honour the memory of his surgeon and he named the nearby island Anderson's Island, it was at latitude 63° 18'. The name did not survive and it became known as St Lawrence Island. It had been discovered by Bering as long ago as 1728. The ships made a landing on another island where they managed to collect some local vegetables for the pot. They also found a sledge about 10 feet long, which they thought at first must have been left by Russian traders but it had no iron in its construction. It was very well made and it was cleverly held together with pins and lashings. It was an Indian construction and they called the island Sledge Island.

They were still making progress to the north when the ships arrived at another cape. The latitude was measured as 65° 46' and when they rounded the cape the land fell away to the east. Cook knew that this was a great moment, he had arrived at long last at the westernmost point on the whole of the American continent, he had proved for the first time that America reached a longitude which he calculated to be 191° 45' E or more correctly 168° 15' W. He called the point of land Cape Prince of Wales. It was a moving moment as the *Resolution* and *Discovery* reached the Bering Straits. The visibility was not good enough to see the coast of Asia but at this point the distance between the two continents was less than 60 miles. Cook decided to sail first to the west before exploring to the north and to try and find land in that direction. The next day he landed, not in America, but on the western extremity of Asia, on the Arctic shores of Siberia.

Even at this freezing northern latitude the country was populated. There were signs of settlement and a village was discovered nearby. It was a village of the Chuckchi people, who were a Mongoloid race from the eastern coast of Asia. Cook was eager to make contact with them and to trade. Cook's account of the meeting stands out as an excellent example of his bravery, his caution and consideration when approaching a new people. One false move and they could easily have killed him, yet he successfully opened up the way for trade and communication:

> As we were standing into this place we perceived on the North shore
> an Indian Village, and some people whom the sight of the Ships
> seemed to have thrown into some confution or fear, as we could see
> some runing inland with burdthens on their backs. To this place I went
> with three Armed boats, accompaned by some of the Officers, and

found 40 or 50 Men each armed with a Spontoon Bow and Arrows
drawn up on a rising ground on which the village stood. As we drew
near three of them came down towards the shore and were so polite as
to take of their Caps and make us a low bow: we returned the
Compliment but this did not inspire them with sufficient confidence
to wait our landing, for the Moment we put the boats a shore they
retired. I followed them alone without any thing in my hand, and by
signs and actions got them to stop and receive some trifles I presented
them with and in return they gave me two fox skins and a couple of Sea
horse teeth. I cannot say whether they or I made the first present, for
these things they brought down with them for this very purpose and
would have given me them without my making any return. They

seemed very fearfull and causious, making signs for no more of our people to come up, and on my laying my hand on one mans Shoulder he started back several paces. In proportion as I advanced they retreated backwards always in the attitude of being ready to make use of their Spears, while those on the hill behind them stood ready to support them with thier arrows. Insensibly my self and two or three more got in amongst them, a few beads distributed to those about us brought on a kind of confidence so that two or three more of our people joining us did not Alarm them, and by degrees a sort of traffick between us commenced.[9]

Knives, beads and tobacco were exchanged, but the Chukchi never dropped their guard. They traded a few arrows but they refused to trade a bow. Webber painted a picture of the scene showing Cook and his men seated in a relaxed fashion amongst their new acquaintances. The village seemed to consist of huts, habitable in the summer and winter quarters sunk into the ground. There were no women or children in the group but they had hunting dogs which were also used to draw their sledges. The stay was only a matter of two or three hours. There was a favourable wind from the south and Cook was eager to get back again to sea and to sail through the Straits of Bering.

Thus, on 13 August, the *Resolution* and *Discovery* passed through the Bering Straits which separated America from Asia. They encountered a calm sea and no ice. They made the obvious decision to follow the America coast, which at this point was running to the north east. The wind was favourable, their luck seemed to be turning at last. Ahead lay a cape, which they called Cape Hope, for hope was certainly aroused in their hearts. Was this then the North West Passage which lay ahead? After many hard months of sailing the high latitudes of the American coast, after so many false alarms, they had eventually rounded the most westerly point of the continent and there was every reason to believe that the passage before them headed across the north of America. The lie of the land was very different from the map published by Stahlin which Cook was still trying desperately to understand. For James

King and many others hopes ran high. They thought they had found the entrance to the North West Passage at long last:

> Which conjecture is right we cannot determine, but we are in high spirits in seeing the land to the No[rth]ward of these Extremitys trend away so far to the NE, and the other NW, which bespeaks an open sea to the No[rth]ward free of land, and we hope of Ice, as we have hitherto seen no signs of any.[10]

The optimists started to calculate the distance to Baffin Bay, and how many days it would take to reach the Atlantic. How many days before they were back again with their loved ones in England? There was still no ice, there was an open sea and there was a fair wind. They had been three years at sea and for seven long months they had searched the forbidding coast of North America. They had been forced to sail further and further to the west to round the icebound coast of Alaska and they had been forced northwards up to nearly 70° of latitude. They well deserved some good fortune at last. The captain, of course, would insist on mapping and charting every part of the passage but they began to count their chickens. They could be back in England before the end of the year.

On 17 August the expedition had reached a latitude of 68° 18' with the coast still heading to the north east. Then there appeared a telling glare in the sky to the north. Cook called it the blink, he had seen the phenomenon before. It was the white reflection from a sheet of ice. The latitude was approaching 70°, he knew that in the Atlantic ships had penetrated to over 80° and still found unfrozen seas in which to sail. But his worst fears were soon upon him. The ice was spotted ahead. At latitude 70° 44' it was just not possible to sail any further, the way forward was blocked by a wall of ice rising to a height of about 10 or 12 feet.

> We now stood to the Southward and after runing Six leagues shoaled the Water to 7 fathoms, which depth continued for near half a mile and

then it deepened to 8 and 9 fathom. At this time the weather which had been very hazey cleared a little and we saw low land extending from South to SEBE about 3 or 4 miles distant. The East extreme form[s] a point which was much incumbered with ice for which Reason it obtained the name of Icey Cape, Lat. 70° 29' N, long. 198° 20' E but the other extreme was lost in the horizon, so that there can be no doubt but it was a continuation of the Amirica continent. The *Discovery* being about a mile astern and to leeward found less water than we did and was obliged to tack for it, which obliged me to tack also for fear of being Separated. Our situation was now more and more critical, we were in shoal water upon a lee shore and the main body of the ice in sight to windward driving down upon us. It was evident, if we remained much longer between it and the land it would force us ashore unless it should happen to take the ground before us; it seemed nearly if not quite to join to the land to leeward and the only direction that was open was to the SW. After making a short board to the Northward I made the Signal for the *Discovery* to tack and tacked my self at the same time. The Wind proved rather favourable so that we laid up SW and SWBW having never less than 10 fathom water, but generally 12 and 13.[11]

It was a bleak reward after months of mapping and charting, of hard and dangerous sailing on an uncharted lee shore, often in shoal water and after all the rats, cockroaches and stale food. They had stuck manfully to their task of exploring the American North West in the hopes of finding the passage. After rounding the whole of the icy wastes of Alaska they had actually found the entrance to the passage. But the key and the entrance to the west was denied them by the solid wall of ice. The only way home to their loved ones could hardly have been a longer and more dangerous journey, it was the other way round the whole world round Cape Horn or the Cape of Good Hope. No men ever deserved their reward more than those of the *Resolution* and *Discovery*. But it was not to be. There was no option but to turn around and go back whence they had come.

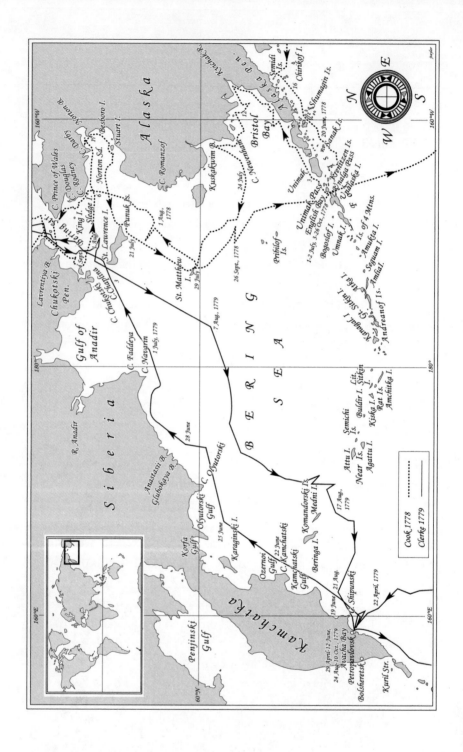

NINE

The Russians

Cook had sailed further north along the west coast of America than any man before him. He had sailed as far as it was possible for his ships to go and a wall of solid ice prevented him from going further. But he was not prepared to give up the search. In his mind he knew it was possible for man to go further still along this inhospitable coastline.

The ships stopped for the night and as they slept the surge and grind of the ice could be heard as the tidal forces caused it to move. To the west was a narrowing passage of water, and Cook speculated that if he had a specially strengthened ship such as those used by the Greenland whalers then it would be possible to break the ice and to progress further into the channel. He pondered on the situation. It was the second half of August and when September came temperatures would begin to fall rapidly. It was simply not safe to continue sailing in a wooden ship any longer under these conditions. It was a great disappointment but all might not quite be lost. He reasoned that in a good summer, if he arrived earlier in the season to give himself August and September to retreat, then it would be possible to penetrate further to the east. Perhaps in a very mild summer he could penetrate far enough to reach the eastern side of America. The expedition was fated to spend another year in the North Pacific. There would be another cold season in the ice. It would be another long year before they even set sail for their homes and for their long-suffering kin. The extra season would make Cook's third voyage of even longer duration than his second voyage in spite of the fact that it would not qualify as a circumnavigation of the earth.

Cook was not prepared to miss out on the other opportunity which now presented itself. He turned back to the west to follow the ice edge. Always the optimist, he thought there was a remote possibility of a passage to the north of Siberia reaching around the Arctic Circle as far as Finland and Norway. If he could find the passage he would follow it as far as it was possible.

For two weeks he sailed westwards at the limit of the ice. On 29 August he met again with the coast of Siberia. He was not really surprised to find that the situation was just the same as on the American side. There was a narrow and dangerous passage of water along the coastline but the ice again presented an impenetrable barrier, this time to the west. The land was bare and inhospitable. It was devoid of human habitation. It was devoid of life. It was devoid even of a blade of grass. The two ships hobbled back along the Siberian coastline and returned again to the Bering Straits. There was little to be gained by loitering longer. There was still one remote possibility. The Russian maps showed the westernmost land on the American continent was an island called Alaschka, disconnected from the American mainland by a large strait and from the Asian continent by a narrow strait. If the map was correct then Cook had navigated the narrow strait and there should still be a wider strait from somewhere further south giving access to the North West Passage.

There was a small consolation to the men in that there was a good supply of fresh meat available inside the Arctic Circle. The walrus, known by the sailors as the sea horse, lay around in great abundance on the ice. It was a simple matter to kill and prepare them for food. The meat was greeted with very mixed reactions, some found the meat revolting and they were unable to stomach it, but others thought it fresh and tasty after the monotonous diet of salted pork and beef.

By September the ships were back on the American coast and they spent another month searching for the passage on Stahlin's map. They explored the inlet at Norton Bay. There was a bulge in the land which turned out to be the delta of the River Yukon. Eventually Cook had no option but to accept that the Russian maps were erroneous. He thought he had identified where the island of Alaschka should be, but it was not an island at all, he could certainly not find a sea passage between the land and the American continent. The *Resolution* was leaking again at the buttocks. As September came to an end he headed across the Bering Sea to the sheltered cove where they had anchored on 1 July. By 3 October they were back at the place called Samganooda where they knew the fishing was good, he also knew that there was a supply of fresh vegetables and trade with the Indian village.

There was another Indian settlement in a bay to the northwards of Samganooda, the people seemed slightly more civilised. Like their neighbours they had flat faces, small noses and eyes with a copper coloured skin. They traded fish and wild berries which they harvested locally. Their houses were not undergound as at Samganooda, but supported by strong upright posts and with cross members and turf walls which were covered with moss to keep the heat in and the cold out. They built a fireplace in the centre of their dwellings for warmth and cooking. They were very polite, they pulled off their caps and made respectful bows to the British. Their hats were decorated with the whiskers of cats, seals and walrus. They also decorated their clothing with beads and feathers. James King noticed that they made small neat images of themselves, carved from bone.

On 8 October there was a curious development. An Indian appeared carrying a rye loaf, which was obviously not a local delicacy. The loaf contained a salmon, perfectly prepared — it had not been traded from the ship and the local Indians could not make bread. The man also brought with him a written note, hidden inside the loaf, and in a language which nobody on the expedition could understand. The British recalled the earlier incident when they passed this way before and one of the sailors was given a wooden whistle with a note inside it. The Indians communicated that the present had come from other

strangers in the area. Somewhere nearby there was another ship or
other explorers or traders and they were attempting to make contact.
The Indians indicated that they were several days travel away but the
bearer of the loaf knew where to find them. After some discussion it
was agreed that Corporal Ledyard of the marines should travel with
the Indians in their canoe to meet with the people who had sent the
note. Ledyard's journey was most uncomfortable. They had to cover a
distance of about 15 miles, mostly on foot but the party of three had
to cross a stretch of water 4 miles wide. The only way to cross was by
canoe. The native canoe was designed for only two people but it was
paddled by two Indians with Corporal Ledyard stowed away between
their feet :

> At one place they were obliged to cross 4 Miles of Water & there being
> only one canoe with Holes for two paddles to sit, the Corporal was
> obliged to suffer himself to be stowed away close in that, which had
> room enough barely to contain him & where he was entirely shut out
> from the Air, tho' he had a little Light for the Skin of the Canoe being
> transparent he could see the Water plain enough, in which he was in a
> manner buryed and only defended from it by thin Leather.[1]

John Ledyard returned a few days later with three Russians. They had
a trading post some miles away and they were trading with the Indians
for skins that they supplied to a market on the Asian coast. It was a
long time since Cook's men had come into contact with civilisation. It
was an historic meeting between two European cultures at one of the
remotest locations on the other side of the world. There was a serious
language barrier but the meeting was recorded by James King:

> The sight of these three Sailors rais'd a peculiar sensation in the breast
> of every one from the Captain downwards which was visible enough in
> our countenances, & in our behaviour towards them. To see people in
> so strange a part of the World who had other ties than that of common
> humanity to recommend them, was such a novelty, & pleasure, & gave

such a turn to our Ideas & feelings as may be very easily imagined. He who we understood to be the Master or Mate of the Vessel was honourd by being the Captains Visitor, whilst we in the Gunroom entertaind the two rough Sailors. We however felt a sensible chagrin that we could understand on[e] another by no common Language; as we expect Visits from other Russians, & some as we understand superior to these, I shall not yet relate what information we contriv'd to get from these our Guests, who left us on the 11th promising to return with a Map of this part of the World.[2]

The Russians had seen the British ships sail by and they had decided to try and make contact. The idea of a loaf with the note inside had succeeded. It was annoying that neither party could understand a word of each other's language but they communicated as best they could with signs and actions. One of the Russian traders, Peter Nat Rubin, claimed to have sailed with Bering's expedition of 1738 but Cook was a little suspicious of his claim for he did not seem old enough. They were hunters and trappers, collecting beaver skins which brought them a very good price on the Asian mainland. They traded with the local Indians for food and supplies, giving them beads, metal objects, tobacco and even snuff. The tobacco was chewed rather than smoked but the Indians thought it a great luxury. James King explained the confusion of the Russians, it is unlikely that Cook was not flying the English Ensign or the Union Flag, it seems more likely that the Russians did not recognise his colours and mistook the two ships for French or Spanish.

The Russians told us that at first they supposed, by the accounts of the Natives, we might be chinese or Japanese: that one of them ventur'd when we were here in July to peep at us over the hills, but that since our last arrival we were taken for Spaniards or French, & that the fear of the last nation made them not venture to trust us; for either from the prejudices to the French, arising from the Assistance they suppose they gave the Turks against their Nation, or from some

extraordinary transaction of which we could make neither head or tale
at Kamchatka, they consider them as their enemies, & say they wou'd
not be permittd to go to St Peter & St Paul, but that we are friends &c.
&c.[3]

The Russians responded to Cook's request for maps and details of the
coast hereabouts and they promised to supply him with his request
and with more information. The three sailors were only an advance
party and five days later, on 15 October, there arrived another Russian.
His name was Erasmin Gregorioff Sin Ismyloff and he seemed to be the
senior person in the area. He arrived in one of the Indian canoes but
which appeared to be his own property, accompanied by two paddlers.
He spoke no English but he understood that the British were there as
a party of exploration and he produced the charts of the area which
Cook had requested. It was only then that Cook found out how erroneous his maps had been. He had wasted months searching for islands
and straits which were pure fiction. He was rightly angered at the
boastful maps of Stahlin and Muller.

In spite of the language problem Cook was able to communicate
well with Ismyloff and he was so pleased with the charts that he
presented the Russian with no less than one of Hadley's quadrants in
recognition of his valuable assistance. He had to explain to the Russian
the purpose of the instrument and how to use it for finding latitude.
Hadley's superb craftsmanship was very obvious to the Russian who
accepted the present with great joy. Ismyloff explained to Cook about
the Russian settlement of St Peter & St Paul (Petropavlovsk) which lay
on the Kamchatka Peninsula in Siberia and was at about the same latitude across the Bering Sea. Cook expressed his interest in visiting the
area and Ismyloff gave him letters of introduction to the governor of
Kamchatka and to the commander of the garrison at Petropavlovsk. It
was a very lucrative meeting. How Cook wished he had met the
Russians a few months earlier on his way to the north.

Cook realised that although they were half the world away from
London, it would be possible to send a communication to the admi-

ralty through the Russian channels via Moscow. He obviously trusted the Russians sufficiently to entrust them with his papers, he knew that it could be almost another year before he had another opportunity to communicate with the admiralty. He had copies made of his maps and charts, with a covering letter to go with them.

It was the end of October. After conferring with the Russians Cook had decided that Alaska was not an island, the Straits of Alashka were a fiction, Alaska was a large forbidding landmass and he was wasting his time searching for a sea passage through it. To the great relief of his men he prepared his ships for the voyage to Hawaii, intending to leave the papers with the traders he had befriended. But just as Cook's ships were ready to leave the harbour another Russian ship appeared. On board was a man called Jacob Ivanovitch, he had heard about the English from the other traders and he had set out to find them. It appeared that he was a superior to Ismyloff and he was the senior Russian in the vicinity. Ivanovitch was the master of the sloop which was to carry Cook's letters and maps on the first stage of their long journey across the whole of Russia to Moscow and eventually to the admiralty in London. He claimed to be a native of Moscow and there seemed no reason to doubt his claim, he seemed even more civilised than Ismyloff. He was very knowledgeable about the geography of the area and Cook showed him the map which his Russian colleague had supplied. Ivanovitch agreed with Ismyloff's geography but not with the glowing account of the Russian settlements on the Kamchatka Peninsula in Siberia.

As they prepared to leave the island they had called Unalashka James King gave a summary of the months they had spent on the American coast and its value to navigation. He gives a great compliment to his commander:

I shall refer to the Map, as much more satisfactory than any written description of this Harbour & Island of Oonalaska, as well as of the adjoining ones, & shall finish with a Vocabulary & our Astronomical Observations; but I cannot leave this Northern Sea, & depart for the

Southern Islands (amongst which I understand we are to spend our
Winter) in another World & amongst a quite different set of Mortals,
without casting an Eye upon what has been done this Summer; here
again a Map will give a better Idea than a description; only I believe I
may venture to say, that there neither was wanting perseverance, skill
nor judgement in our Commander, or rather that they were never
surpass'd in such like services; & that during one Summer, an extent
of Coast of above 1100 Leagues was examin'd & pretty accurately
survey'd, not taking into account the large part of the NEern coast of
Asia that we sail'd along.[4]

King was realistic enough to see however, that the chances of success
in the next season were not good. He did not agree with Cook's decision to spend another year searching for the North West Passage. It is
probable that the majority of the officers and crew agreed with King
but not one of them dared to voice their opinion to the captain. James
King put his private thoughts into his journal. They had penetrated
71° to the north and in spite of the long and slow survey of 1,100
leagues of coastline their timing was almost perfect in the sense that
they arrived at the ice wall at the end of August. The seasons obviously had a wide variation but July and August were the warmest
months and the ice had receded to its maximum by the start of
September. It was very unlikely that the ice would have receded any
further by the next season and even if it did then they had no idea how
much further they had to sail before reaching more temperate climes.
It was true that they had encountered mild weather in September when
they returned to Norton Sound but King reasoned that they had been
in a sheltered spot with the mountains shielding the bay from the
worst of the northerly winds.

There was much discussion about the nature of the ice. Many of the
officers still held with the theory that sea water could not freeze. The
erroneous theory was that the ice was created from fresh water in the
rivers and the icebergs were carried down to the sea by the river water.
Wind and current were thought to carry the icebergs to the ice shelf to

the north which created the barrier to their progress. Some argued that at latitude 65° the two continents were only 13 leagues apart but at 69° north they were at least 100 leagues apart. It seemed that the further north they could sail the more water existed. The optimists argued that early in the season there would be less ice, for the rivers had not brought down the seasonal crop of icebergs. But James King rejected this theory. The Siberian rivers were too shallow to bring large icebergs to the Arctic Sea and the depth of the ice shelf was very obvious:

> The body of Ice was far too deep, even the detatchd pieces were; besides we should have seen some sign of Earth, or some produce of the banks of the rivers upon some of the bodys, whereas it seem'd as if it had been froze, & upon its frozen surface great bodies of Snow had fallen, which also became froze & added to the Mass. The different colour in most of the Masses could not be well accountd for otherwise: but it is not the Plan of a log to argue from appearances, but simply to note them; I shall not often Err in this respect.[5]

James Cook was satisfied that he had gained all the information he could from the Russian traders. It was the end of October and the nights were drawing in. The state of the ships was terrible and in other circumstances they would not have been allowed to put to sea. There was no option. The two leaky ships with their worn sails, their rotten and leaky hulls and battered rigging, had to sail to Hawaii to winter there. Then they had still to face the terrible journey to the frozen north for the second season, to penetrate as far as it was possible for man to go. If their mission failed a second time, and hardly a man on board still believed that a passage to the west existed, then they had to face the long and dangerous journey home through practically all of the world's great oceans.

TEN

Hawaii

It was now that the good fortune of the new discovery in the previous year came into its own. The *Resolution* and *Discovery* turned to the south where they knew there existed the archipelago of Hawaii which was the ideal place to spend a winter season in the warm climate. There could hardly have been a sharper contrast than that between the frozen wastes of Alaska and the tropical paradise of Hawaii. There was a delay of about four days when the ships were hit by unpredictable storms from all points of the compass and at one point the main tack of the *Discovery* gave way and one seaman, John McIntosh from Perth, was lost. Except for these incidents the journey south was uneventful. Captain Cook made sure that there were no idle hands. The spun yarn winch came into action to recycle the worn out rigging and as the days became warmer the deck was the place where the sails were laid out for repair. The carpenters were busy replacing rotten timbers and there was always caulking of the seams to be done somewhere on the ships. Every day saw the latitude down by another degree. Every day saw the average temperature a degree warmer.

By the end of November the ships had crossed the tropic of Cancer and they had reached the right latitude for the Hawaiian Islands. The course was planned to take them to the longitude of Kauai but the unpredictable weather carried them about 4° to the east and when dawn broke on 27 November the explorers found themselves near the island of Maui. They could not fail to be impressed with the great volcanic cone of Haleakala rising steeply out of the water to a height of over 3,000 metres. In the distance, but above the horizon, was an even larger peak. The great double peak of Mauna Kea was rising more than 4,000 metres from sea level, so high that even in the tropics the upper slopes were as white with snow as the frozen peaks they had left behind in Alaska.

There soon appeared the houses and the plantations and the dark-skinned people who came out to trade in their canoes. Not many of the Hawaiians had seen the *Resolution* and *Discovery* in the short visit the previous year and they were prancing with excitement at seeing the two large ships entering their waters.   Soon excited islanders were clambering all over the decks and for a time all went well. Then James Cook began to behave in a very uncharacteristic fashion. The trade was good and there was no problem with the food supplies, the only problem was the shortage of iron and other things for barter, but even this had not reached a crisis point. Cook sent landing parties ashore for fresh water but he did not attempt to make a landing himself, only the watering party were allowed on land. His face was set and grim. He did not feel it necessary to explain his conduct to his officers or his men.

He issued a set of strict orders, no firearms were to be taken ashore and no women were to be allowed on the ship. The crew complained, and with good reason. Not only did they feel they had earned their right to enjoy the native girls but they were still kept on short rations when the trading meant that fresh food was plentiful again. Cook immediately increased their rations, his excuse was simply that he had forgotten to give the necessary order, but he was not in a co-operative or communicative mood. He wrote a long grouching letter to the admiralty complaining about the state of his rigging and claiming that private vessels in the merchant service had better rigging than he could obtain for his voyages of three or four years' duration:

On this occasion I cannot help observing, that I have always found that the bolt-ropes to our sails have not been of sufficient strength, or substance to even half wear out the Canvas: this at different times has been the occasion of much expence of canvas and infinate trouble and vexation Nor are the cordage and canvas or indeed hardly any other stores made use of in the Navy, of equal goodness with those in general used in the Merchant service, of this I had incontestable proof last voyage. When the *Resolution* was purchased for the King her standing rigging, some runing rigging, blocks and sails were also purchased along with her, and altho the most of these things had been in wear fourteen Months yet they wore longer than any of those of the same kind put on board new out of the Kings stores. The fore rigging are yet over the mast head, the brace blocks and some others in equal use still in their places and as good as ever. And yet on my return home last voyage these very blocks were condemned by the yard officers and thrown amongst other decayed blocks from which they permited my Boatswain to select them when the ship was again fited out. These evils are likely never to be redressed, for besides the difficulty of procuring stores for the Crown of equal goodness with [those] purchased by private people for their own use, it is a general received opinion amongst Naval officers of all ranks that no stores are equal in goodness to those of the Crown and that no ships are found like those of the Navy. In the latter They are right but it is in the quantity and not in the quallity of the stores, this last is seldom tried, for things are generally Condemned or converted to some other use by such time as they are half wore out. It is only on such Voyages as these we have an oppertunity to make the trial where every thing is obliged to be worn to the very utmost.[1]

When Christmas Day arrived there was still no attempt to land anywhere. It was spent at sea. It was a whole year on from Christmas Island and two years on from Kerguelen. Cook did not record the event in his journal but when we read Samwell's account we find that on the *Discovery* there was a drunken running battle between the decks, one poor Hawaiian who had the misfortune to be on board at the time was in terror of his life. Samwell's account does not sound like one of Cook's well ordered ships:

> We are out of Sight of the Island to standing to Eastward, being Christmas day it was kept by the People according to ancient usage from time immemorial. At night there was a general battle among them between decks and the poor Indian was hemmed in in the thickest of them; one of the Gent[leme]n seeing him, with great difficulty got him out. The poor fellow was in the utmost Terror & apprehension tho' no one had offered to touch him; as it is naturel to suppose, such a scene of Uproar & Confusion must strike him, & he no doubt looked upon them all, as a parcell of Madmen & was glad to escape from their fury.[2]

An important chief came out to visit. His name was Terryaboo and a deck full of attendants accompanied him. He was an old man of about sixty, red eyed and weak, he was befuddled by drink but he was amiable and friendly. He presented Cook with a valuable cap of yellow and black feathers and also a feather cloak. Terryaboo wanted Cook to land on his island and he suggested an anchorage to the east. Cook was not interested, he had his eye on the larger island of O'why'he or Hawaii. He made the approach to the island but even when the days of tacking around turned into weeks he had still made no effort to find a place where he could land. His officers and his men were understandably very unhappy with the situation, they were fed up with cruising around on the edge of paradise and not being given any reason why they could not land. Cook was operating a deliberate policy of delay. Nothing could be more frustrating for men who had so recently suffered many months of icy seas in search of the North West Passage. Captain Cook seemed more interested in things other than exploration, he discovered that a tolerable beer could be brewed from the local sugar cane and he assumed that it would be highly esteemed by everybody on board. He had some of the beer made and offered it to the crew, it would enable him to cut back on the ration of spirits and to preserve them for the next season in search of the North West Passage. Not one of the crew would even taste the so called beer. Cook described the incident in his journal. It was a passage which reads quite out of character. When had James Cook ever before used such hard words as 'my mutinous crew' and 'turbulent crew' for the men under his command?

> Having procured a quantity of Sugar Cane and had upon trial made but a few days before, found that a strong decoction of it made a very palatable beer, which was esteemed by every one on board, I ordered some more to be brewed, but when the Cask came to be broached not one of my Mutinous crew would even so much as taste it. As I had no motive for doing it but to save our spirit for a Colder climate, I gave my self no trouble either to oblige or persuaid them to drink it, knowing there was no danger of the Scurvy so long as we had plenty of other Vegetables; but that I might not be disapointed in my views I gave orders that no grog should be served in either Ship. My self and the Officers continued to make use of this beer whenever we could get cane to make it; a few hops, of which we had on board, was a great addition to it: it has the taste of new malt beer, and I beleive no one will d[o]ubt but it must be very wholesom, though my turbulent crew alleged it was injurious to their healths.[3]

Things went from bad to worse. When William Griffin opened a cask of sour beer Cook gave him the severe punishment of twelve lashes on the grounds that he had no right to open it. The offence required a naval punishment, but this was not the humane captain of the *Endeavour* voyage.

The New Year was upon them but still there was no landing. When Cook was pressed by his officers to justify his actions he regaled them with an account of the trade position. He forwarded the argument that the trade was necessary, when the canoes came out to trade then some of the produce must be bought otherwise the locals would not come out to trade again. The result was a great surplus of food such as fresh fruit and vegetables, which was ideal for a scurvy free diet, but much of it decayed after a few days and had to be thrown overboard. The nails and knives needed for barter were scarce and he was afraid that a time would come when there would be nothing left with which to purchase supplies. By keeping out to sea it was difficult for the canoes to reach the ships and he was able to control and limit the amount of trade. Another aspect which Cook does not mention was the amount of time they had to kill, there was no point in sailing from Hawaii until the spring months at the earliest and he wanted to be sure that he did not outstay his welcome.

He sailed his ships around the big island of Hawaii. He claimed to be searching for a harbour but he was so far offshore that he was unable to assess the suitability of any harbour they could see. The weather was admittedly very heavy and the winds were unpredictable and variable so that it was dangerous to go in too close for fear that a sudden change in the wind could carry the ships onto the coral rocks. At one point he was nearly caught out by a change in the wind, orders were urgently yelled out to change tack. It was a very close call and he just managed to clear the next headland without striking the rocks. The two ships generally managed to keep together but on one occasion Cook changed tack without making the signal to the *Discovery*. The consort did not change tack and the two became separated for several days. They eventually met again having sailed in opposite directions around the island.

The mutterings and the idle talk of mutiny continued below decks and Cook ran out of excuses. He knew that he must make a landing soon. A possible place was Kealakekua Bay on the south west coast of Hawaii Island. The islanders, when they realised the great ships were at last approaching the land, came out in great numbers to greet them. As many as a thousand canoes appeared and the trade was very brisk indeed. James King estimated that as many as ten thousand people had come to welcome them. The Hawaiians climbed onto the ships in great numbers and at one point there were so many on the *Discovery* that she nearly heeled over. It was the local chiefs who saved the situation by ordering the climbers to drop off the ship to be collected by the canoes. Then a long line of canoes appeared from the north point of the bay. It was a ceremonial procession to welcome the new arrivals. James Burney gives a description:

> The Ships were accompanied into the Harbour by an immense Fleet of Canoes, near 800, according to those who took the pains to count, the people on board these, were not more numerous than those who having no Canoes, swam off to us from the Shore as soon as we Anchord. the Numbers being too great to admit all Visitors none but females were at first allowed entrance, and with those the Ship soon became so thronged, that many hundreds were obliged to be drove overboard, to make room for carrying on the necessary duty of the Ship: and it was constant employment for a fourth part of the Ships company to keep the decks clear.[4]

The account agrees with Cook who described his own view of the situation:

> I have no where in this Sea seen such a number of people assembled at one place, besides those in the Canoes all the Shore of the bay was covered with people and hundreds were swiming about the Ships like shoals of fish. We should have found it difficult to have kept them in order had not a Chief or Servant of Terrioboos named Palea now and then [exerted] his authority by turning or rather driving them all out of the Ships. Among our numerous Visitors was a man named Tou-ah-ah, who we soon found belonged to the Church, he introduced himself with much ceremony, in the Course of which he presented me with a small pig, two Cocoanuts and a piece of red cloth which he wraped round me: in this manner all or most of the chiefs or people of Note interduce them selves, but this man went farther, he brought with him a large hog and a quant[it]y of fruits and roots all of which he included in the present. In the after noon I went a shore to view the place,

accompanied by Touahah, Parea, Mr King and others; as soon as we landed Touahah took me by the hand and conducted me to a large Morai, the other gentlemen with Parea and four or five more of the Natives followed.[5]

At last Captain Cook set foot upon the island of Hawaii. He was accompanied by King and Bayly. The people rejoiced to see him and a man called Koa, who seemed to be the chief priest of the island, took him by the hand, wrapped a sacred red cloth around him and led him to what appeared to be a shrine or temple to one of the island gods. There was something about his reception which was very different from anything in his previous experience. He was led to what was obviously a very sacred place, a paved rectangle about 40 yards long and 20 yards wide. There were two huts with two wooden images. Nearby was a kind of scaffolding tower made from poles and sticks. There was an altar where a pig had been sacrificed with a variety of fruits set around it. They were received by a chief called Keli'ikea who uttered a prayer and asked Cook to climb the rickety scaffolding to the tower. Keli'ikea conducted a ceremony around a semi-circle of images which seemed to be local gods. He prostrated himself to a small image in the centre and kissed it. Cook was required to do the same. Cook was then seated between the images and he was brought an offering of baked hog and other provisions. There were more speeches and incantations with the word 'Erono' chanted and repeated again and again. Then the company sat down to eat. The hog was putrid and Captain Cook had no appetite at all for it, but Keli'ikea politely chewed it for him to make it more palatable — the captain was still unable to digest it!

When the feast was over the party made a ceremonial walk around the houses and back to the shore. They were preceded by wand bearers. By this time there could be no doubt about the meaning of the ritual. The Hawaiians had decided that Captain Cook was a god who had arrived from another world to visit them.

Cook made no objections. He played his part as the god Erono whilst his men obtained the supplies they needed. The worship was also extended to Captain Clerke, whom they could see was his second in command and to his lieutenant James King. Clerke was very uncomfortable at being treated as a god, he would have nothing to do with it and told the natives to desist. King was also uncomfortable and he avoided the situation as much as possible.

As Captain Cook passed by the people fell to the ground and chanted the word 'Erono', wherever he went they were falling at his feet as he passed. Cook appeared to take it all in his stride. His crew were respected and well treated. The supply of food was plentiful. It was possible for the rest of the crew to get on with other business. The rudder of the *Discovery* was taken ashore for repairs. Carpenters went inland to cut timber. The blacksmith was busier than anybody trying to refurnish new tools from old iron and he furnished some long iron daggers which became valuable items of trade. They were coveted by the Hawaiians as far superior to their own wooden daggers.

Now that a landing had been made at last it was possible for the society and the customs of the people to be studied. The boxing and wrestling sports were similar to those on the other Polynesian island groups but subtly different on account of the variation of the cultures. The British seamen were unacquainted with the boxing and wrestling rules and after their drubbing at the Tonga Isles they wisely refrained from joining in with the sport:

> In the afternoon the Indians exhibited some boxing matches on a level piece of Ground a little way from the Tents. An oblong square was formed by the People, at the bottom of which were displayed three Ensigns or whatever else they may be called, they are made of a long pole with a stick about a Yard & a half long made fast at the upper end of it so as to form a Cross, to this stick are hung pieces of Cloth of various Colours with a few red Feathers, two or three Geese & other birds, forming upon the whole a picture like that in Hudibras in the Cavalcade to Hornfair. Before two Combatants met, a man at the upper end of the Ring repeated some words & was answered by all the People at the lower end who stood round the Ensign, on which some

Man immediately advanced into the ring who soon met with his antagonist; they approached each other slowly, at the same time lifts up
their feet behind & drawing their hands along the Soles of them to
gather the dust, intended probably to prevent them from being slip-
pery & to give them a firmer gripe. They examine each other with
their Eyes from head to foot & generally give themselves some affected
airs, by staring round with an arch look, shrugging their Shoulders &c.
This they do when they meet as well as when the battle is over. They
advance holding out both Arms in a strait line before their faces, at
which part they aim all their blows; they keep no manner of Guard but
avoid the adversary's blow by retreating, they do not strike with a
strait arm but with the whole swing of it, so that it would be an easy
matter for any of our expert boxers to break their arms or disable
them; the battle is soon decided, whenever one of them was knocked
down or fell he gave up and the other turned his backside to him and
gave himself other airs of Triumph, or rather of affectation, which
generally excited a laugh among the Spectators; he did not go off the
field but waited for another Antagonist and often staid till he was
conquered by a succession of them if the second did not succeed.[6]

We cannot pass by Hawaii without describing one of the pastimes for
which it became famous. David Samwell watched with amazement at
the way the young children played without fear in the great curling
white breakers of the beach. He described the idyllic island of Hawaii,
still in its pristine form, with a description of surfing long before it was
taken up by the western world:

As two or three of us were walking along shore to day we saw a number
of boys & young Girls playing in the Surf, which broke very high on
the Beach as there was a great swell rolling into the Bay. In the first
place they provide themselves with a thin board about six or seven foot
long & about 2 broad, on these they swim off shore to meet the Surf,
as soon as they see one coming they get themselves in readiness & turn
their sides to it, they suffer themselves to be involved in it & then

manage so as to get just before it or rather on the Slant or declivity of the Surf, & thus they lie with their Hands lower than their Heels laying hold of the fore part of the board which receives the force of the water on its under side, & by that means keeps before the wave which drives it along with an incredible Swiftness to the shore. The Motion is so rapid for near the Space of a stones throw that they seem to fly on the water, the flight of a bird being hardly quicker than theirs. On their putting off shore if they meet with the Surf too near in to afford them a tolerable long Space to run before it they dive under it with the greatest Ease & proceed further out to sea. Sometimes they fail in trying to get before the surf, as it requires great dexterity & address, and after struggling awhile in such a tremendous wave that we should have judged it impossible for any human being to live in it, they rise on the other side laughing and shaking their Locks & push on to meet the next Surf when they generally succeed, hardly ever being foiled in more than one attempt. Thus these People find one of their Chief amusements in that which to us presented nothing but Horror & Destruction, and we saw with astonishment young boys & Girls about 9 or ten years of age playing amid such tempestuous Waves that the hardiest of our seamen would have trembled to face, as to be involved in them among the Rocks, on which they broke with a tremendous Noise, they could look upon as no other than certain death. So true it is that many seeming difficulties are easily overcome by dexterity & Perseverance.[7]

Now that Captain Cook was established as a god there were, as usual, plenty of local girls willing to confer their sexual favours. The cost was a ship's nail and these were in short supply, giving rise to serious problems for the ships. It was not unknown for sailors to draw the nails from the ship's timbers in order to pay for a night with one of the Hawaiian girls. This was of course a serious offence and they knew that the captain would punish them with the lash if they were discovered. But nails were drawn not only from the inside of the ship but from the outside as well. The natives wanted the iron and they thought they had every right to help themselves. Some made an ingenious tool like a claw for drawing the nails from the hull of the ship, it was a short stick with a flint fixed at one end. Charles Clerke, when he discovered the problem, fired small shot at the thieves in the hope of scaring them away, but they were expert swimmers and they swam beneath the ship out of reach. They did not seem to appreciate that they were doing any wrong in stealing the nails. The thieving was generally not as bad as at Tahiti but there were many similar incidents. It was the iron and other metals which they coveted more than anything:

> ...the Night before our getting here the *Resolution* lost the Lids of the Ships Coppers which were conveyed out of the Ship by some Visitors who were allowed to sleep on board. the Morning we Anchord, almost all our Backstay Tackles were cut out of the Chains, for the Sake of the Iron Hooks and Thimbles, and carried off. Several other things which were part of the Ship's Furniture, went the same way.[8]

The terrible condition of the ship's cordage and rigging was made even worse by the thieving. Burney claims that the decks were so leaky they could not be scrubbed:

> Our present business, besides Watering and procuring Refreshments, was to repair the Sails and Rigging, Caulk the Ship and take in Ballast, from the length of our late Cruize the Ship was in a most tattered condition and her upper works so leaky that we had been obliged to leave off washing Decks for the last 3 Weeks.— 'Burney M, 17 January.'[9]

On 3 February there was another death. It was that of William Watman, he was a middle-aged man who had sailed on Cook's second voyage and he had followed his captain from retirement at Greenwich Hospital to go on the third voyage. The Hawaiians understood the need for a ceremonial burial and he was allowed to be buried on shore. Watman was forty-four and was considered an old man, but the oldest man on the expedition was the captain who had passed his fiftieth birthday the previous October.

Cook only enjoyed the experience of being a god for eighteen days. On 4 February the ships were ready to sail on and some of the priests, jealous of the status which had been given to Cook and his men, were pleased to see the preparations for departure. The *Resolution* and the *Discovery* weighed anchor and sailed from Kealakekua Bay to the usual escort of native canoes.

After only three days at sea an old problem reappeared. It was the fore mast of the *Resolution*, the one with the rotten cheeks which had been replaced at Nootka Sound the previous year. The mast support had given way again, the replacement cheeks fitted at Nootka Sound had fared even worse than the originals and they had both split. It was necessary to find somewhere to repair the mast. The ship could have struggled on to another island but they knew that the place they had just left had an anchorage and suitable timber. They decided to return again to Kealakekua Bay from whence they had just come, the other alternatives involved too many unknown factors.

It was 11 February when the ships returned to Kealakekua Bay after only one week at sea. The local people were surprised and confused to see the ships return, particularly when they were told the reason. There was an uncomfortable feeling in the air. It was hard to put a finger on it — but the return of the ships was not welcomed by some of the priests. Why had the god returned? The season for Erono was over. Some of the islanders certainly did not believe Captain Cook to be a deity, for if he was a god then he could repair the ship without coming back to the island. Surely they thought, if Erono was truly a god then his ships would not suffer from mortal problems. Cook sensed the unease and he armed the marines but he insisted that they loaded their muskets with grapeshot and not musket balls.

It took two days to take out the troublesome fore mast. By 13 February the carpenters had the mast on shore and they were busy working on it. The work was strangely unmolested by natives and there was hardly a canoe in sight. This was because the chiefs had ordered a tapu on the bay. The carpenters had kept back some hard timber from the island of Moorea and this was chosen to make the new fishplates for the mast. Some of the Hawaiians were helping to fill the water casks with the quartermaster William Hollamby in charge but, although they were rewarded for their services, after a time they became insolent. Hollamby was worried by this turn of events and he asked Lieutenant King for a marine guard. The guard, a single marine who was under orders not to fire, was totally ineffective, his presence only seemed to anger the onlookers and they began to throw stones. James King appealed to the chiefs to stop the stoning. The chiefs co-operated, they drove away the troublemakers and there was peace again. King reported the incident to Cook. The captain was concerned, he ordered that the muskets were to be used if it happened again, this time loaded with ball instead of shot.

On the *Discovery* a man had stolen the tongs from the armourer's forge. The tongs were returned half an hour later and the thief was caught. He was given the severe punishment of forty lashes in the hope that it would deter further thefts. To try and prevent another such incident Charles Clerke turned all the Hawaiians off his ship except the chiefs, but neither the punishment nor the banishing had any effect. On this day chief Terryaboo had just left the *Discovery*, and Palea (or Parea) was in the captain's cabin with Clerke. A thief climbed over the side and made off with the same tongs and a chisel from the armourer's forge; he made off in Palea's canoe. Why was it that the tongs were stolen for a second time? The Hawaiians had been trying hard to work the metals themselves but with only limited success. They saw magic in the armourer's tongs which were used to fashion implements from iron. Clerke fired muskets after the thief but it was too late so he sent Thomas Edgar and George Vancouver in a boat to retrieve the stolen items. The two men left in such a hurry that they had no time to collect their firearms to take with them. They did not manage to catch up with the canoe but as they reached the shore another canoe came out to greet them carrying the missing tongs, the chisel and a copper lid which they did not know had been stolen from a water cask.

This should have been the end of the incident but then two unfortunate things happened. Cook and King, who at the time were on shore
dealing with the observatory, had heard firing and they saw a chase —
they knew that something of value had been stolen and they set off to
intercept the thief. Many others had heard the firing and by this time
a great crowd had collected on the beach. Cook, accompanied by a
single marine and separated from King, was directed in the wrong
direction by one of the natives. He did not realise that the stolen items
had been returned. There was no godly veneration from the onlookers
as he was forced to walk back to the boat after being sent on a wild
goose chase. The mob began to laugh at the way he had been misled.
They knew that they were dealing with mere mortals. They knew that
they had the upper hand and that the British were greatly outnumbered.

By this time Palea had left the *Discovery* and he was on shore making
a show of helping the British. When Edgar saw Palea's canoe he knew
that the stolen items had been returned but, acting on his own initia-
tive, he decided to seize the canoe to make an example out of the
thieves. The scene quickly escalated into violence and stoning:

I took the paddle from him, he then came behind me, and while I was
putting the Canoe off a second time he Seized on me, when one of the
pinnace men, seeing this, up with his Oar & Struck Par-rea [Palea] on
the Head, at that Inst a Shower of Stones came from about 2 or 3
hundred People on a Rising Ground, & soon after Closed on the
Pinnace, she being aground Aft, which forced the Crew to leave the
Boat & Swim off to some Rock's a little distance, where our small
Cutter took them in; all this time some of the Natives was Stoneing &
beating the Midshipman and me, while the rest was Stealing the Oar's
& furniture belonging to the Boat. I not being able to swim had got
upon a small rock up to my knees in water, when a man came up with
a broken Oar, and most certainly would have knock'd me off the rock,
into the water, if Mr Vancover, the Midshipman, had not at that Inst

Step'd out of the Pinnace, between the Indian & me, & receiv'd the
Blowe, which took him on the side, & knock'd him down.[10]

This was not the end of the incident. Edgar was taken forcibly by three
men to see Palea, he had made a serious error of judgement and he
thought he could rely on firepower support from the marines. The
chief seemed to be doing his utmost to ease the situation and to
prevent it from escalating, he returned a broken oar and escorted Edgar
back to the boat where the Hawaiians were trying to remove the metal
fitments:

Another Indian came & beat me with a flat piece of board, which soon
Split, when Par-rea came up to us and orderd the Mob to Desist & told
us to go off with our Boat, but the Oar's being all stole prevented us,
he told us he would go & fetch them, and soon as he was gone the Mob
begun again & seeing them all arming themselves with stones, I told
the Midshipman it was not safe staying there, after Par-rea was gone.
I told him to follow me, when I got up the Rocks I intended going
towards Capt: Cooke, but was prevented by three men, who laid hold
of me, & told me I should go to Par-rea; being in their power I
submitted & went to them, when we came to a little Town they made
me stop, & soon after I saw Par-rea and another man coming with an
Oar & a broken one; when Par-rea came up to us, he told me to go back
with him, when we came to the Pinnace I found the Midshipman there,
who told me after I went away the Indians came & knock'd him down.
Stole his Cap & was Striving to knock the ring bolts out of the Stem
& Stern of the Boat; we call'd the small Cutter in who had been all this
time laying off out of Stones throw, we put off with the Pinnace &
Cutter, and Row'd towards the Tents with both Boats to Acquaint
Capt: Cooke of what had happned, on our way there Par-rea came after
us in a Canoe & brought with him Mr Vancovers Cap, and Ask'd if he
should come on board in the morning whether we should not hurt him
for what had happned, we answerd in the Neggative he then left us &
Paddled over for the Town call'd Kavaroa, soon after we met with

Capt: Cooke, when I acquainted him of what had happned, and then came on board.[11]

Edgar and Vancouver escaped back to the ship in the pinnace. Vancouver lost his cap in the mêlée but Palea retrieved it and followed the men back to the *Discovery* to return the property. Cook was furious with Edgar for taking the law into his own hands. It was a terrible mistake for Edgar to attack Palea, who seemed to be the most co-operative of the chiefs, the man who had retrieved the stolen property and had stopped the stoning incident on the previous day. Cook was afraid that the Hawaiians would realise how vulnerable he and his men were. Their confidence had been broken and there was much discontent. He felt that he would at last be obliged to use force to show them that they could gain no advantage.

The night was not without incident. James King was in charge of the observatory tent on shore. A few men came creeping up on the tent and a nervous sentry fired one shot. There was a much more serious incident in the middle of the night. The *Discovery's* large cutter was stolen by stealth — the mooring rope was cut right through. In the morning Clerke went straight to the *Resolution* to tell Cook what had happened. The British could not afford to ignore the theft, the cutter was the largest boat the ship had and it was essential to get it back again. It was decided to seize all the canoes in the bay and to set up a blockade to prevent anybody leaving the bay until the cutter was returned and John Rickman was put in charge of a party of marines to hold the south point of the bay. James King arrived on board to report on events from the observatory but he was sent back on shore to calibrate the chronometer. Cook thought it wise to go to chief Terryaboo who was also known as Kalei'opu'u, on the main island of Hawaii, to explain about the theft and to make a plea for general peace. He took with him Molesworth Phillips and nine marines, all carrying loaded muskets. His plan was to take the chief Terryaboo as a hostage until the cutter was returned. Captain Cook had spent much time avoiding bloodshed and keeping his men from using their firearms. Williamson had killed a Hawaiian on the first landing the previous year, but this was an isolated incident and the natives knew little about the lethal power of the muskets. Some of Cook's officers thought it best to kill one or two men as an example to scare the rest. Cook hated this idea and he firmly resisted it.

Captain Cook marched into the village, with an armed escort of marines under Molesworth Phillips, where he found Terryaboo's two young sons. It was still early morning and the boys took Molesworth Phillips to their father's hut. The chief had only just woken up but he claimed to know nothing of the stolen cutter. Terryaboo was quite happy to accompany Cook and the marines to the ship and as the party set off a great crowd gathered around them. They had reached the shore when the chief's wife and two others ran after them and began to argue, they told Terryaboo he was going to be killed.

It was then that things began to turn ugly. The crowd was growing in numbers all the time and they were restless and angry. On the captain's orders the marines formed a line to face them. Many of the Hawaiians were armed with spears and daggers, including the metal daggers supplied by the ship's armoury. The launch was in the bay under the command of John Williamson, as was the cutter under William Lanyon, and the pinnace under Henry Roberts.

It was obvious to Cook that there was no way to get his hostage on board without creating a scene and wounding or even killing several people, but there was nothing to stop him walking down to the boats and returning to the ship without Terryaboo. He began slowly to make his way to the boats when two things happened at the same time.

Muskets had been fired at the end of the bay by John Rickman and others, they had been posted at the south point of the bay to hold back any canoes. A man had been killed, his name was Kalimu and he was a chief of high rank. Another chief hastened to the ships to tell Cook of the killing, but he was redirected to the beach instead. Thus it transpired that the crowd got the news of the killing before it reached Cook. They were already in a great state of excitement and the news caused them to attack Cook's party. The captain was threatened with

a dagger and a stone. Cook fired one barrel of his musket, loaded with
small shot, at his attacker. The shot did no damage for the man carried
a heavy protective mat as armour, but the incident enraged the
Hawaiians. Terryaboo's young son had climbed into the boat on his
own, but the angry scene had made him very frightened and he scrambled back ashore. One of the Hawaiians attempted to stab Molesworth
Phillips. Stones were hurled and a marine was knocked down. Cook
fired his other barrel and killed a man. Phillips fired his musket. The
crowd came forward to attack. Cook ordered the other marines to fire.
Phillips had reloaded his musket but the other marines did not have
time. Cook then shouted to everybody to get to the boats but Phillips
had been knocked down by a stone and had been stabbed in the
shoulder. He shot his assailant dead and scrambled into the boat, but
then he had to climb out again to save a drowning colleague. Phillips
lost sight of Cook but the men in the pinnace could see him.

Cook was left by himself on the rocks. James Cleveley, a carpenter
on the *Resolution*, had some talent as a draughtsman and he made
sketches of the scene that his brother John Cleveley later made into a
series of pictures. Cleveley's picture of Cook's last moments show him
fighting for his life and using his musket as a club — a very different
interpretation to what later became the official view of James Cook the
peacemaker rather than James Cook the warrior. Samwell described the
final moments of Cook's life:

Captain Cook was now the only Man on the Rock, he was seen walking
down towards the Pinnace, holding his left hand against the Back of
his head to guard it from the Stones & carrying his Musket under the
other Arm. An Indian came running behind him, stopping once or
twice as he advanced, as if he was afraid that he should turn round,
then taking him unaware he sprung to him, knocked him on the back
of his head with a large Club taken out of a fence, & instantly fled
with the greatest precipitation; the blow made Captain Cook stagger
two or three paces, he then fell on his hand & one knee & dropped his
Musket, as he was rising another Indian came running to him & before

he could recover himself from the Fall drew out an iron Dagger he concealed under his feathered Cloak & stuck it with all his force into the back of his Neck, which made Capt. Cook tumble into the Water in a kind of a bite by the side of the rock where the water is about knee deep; here he was followed by a croud of people who endeavoured to keep him under water, but struggling very strong with them he got his head up & looking towards the Pinnace which was not above a boat hook's Length from him waved his hands to them for Assistance, which it seems it was not in their Power to give. The Indians got him under water again but he disengaged himself & got his head up once more & not being able to swim he endeavoured to scramble on the Rock, when a fellow gave him a blow on the head with a large Club and he was seen alive no more. They now kept him under water, one man sat on his Shoulders & beat his head with a stone while others beat him with Clubs & Stones, they then hauled him up dead on the Rocks where they stuck him with their Daggers, dashed his head against the rock & beat him with Clubs & Stones...[12]

The account of Cook's death is close to the truth. Captain Cook was close to the lava edge waving the boats to come in to assist when he was hit from behind with the club. He staggered forward. Then he was stabbed in the neck with an iron dagger made in his own forge. He fell face down in the water. There was a great shout from the crowd and a rush to finish him off with daggers and clubs. The pinnace was commanded by John Williamson who misunderstood Cook's signal, he stood off and moved further out instead of going in to help. The cutter came round and fired at the crowd until she was recalled to the ship. The *Resolution* then fired her four-pounders and the sudden thunder of the large guns sounded across the bay. It frightened the crowd and they fell away. Four marines and Captain Cook lay dead.

There was a deathly silence in Kealakekua Bay.

ELEVEN

The Voyage Home

There was no time to grieve.

The thunder of the great guns had caused the crowd to run in terror from the bay. The launch and the small cutter went in to assess the situation. The bodies could easily have been recovered but Samwell explained that the change in the situation was so very sudden that the men were too bewildered and confused to do anything:

The Launch kept a fire from the Situation she was in on the Indians on shore, at the same time the officer gave Orders for the small Cutter to go close in shore with four or five youngsters in her & keep a fire on the Indians; they went close in but could hardly find an Indian to fire at, there being only a few Stragglers thinly scatter'd here & there, & the dead Bodies of Captn Cook and the four Marines lying on the rock close to the water's edge with only two or three Indians about them, so that there could be no manner of difficulty in taking them in. However one or two muskets having got wet in the Launch & ab[ou]t as many men saying that their Cartridges were almost expended, this was thought a sufficient excuse for returning to the Ship & leave the dead body of their great Commander exposed on the beach to the insults & Barbarities of the Indians. What can be said to this! — they did return on board with the Boats with about forty men in them, the

major part of whom according to their own declaration had their boxes
nearly full, not having expended above 3 or four Cartridges; as they
were pulling off, the Coxswain of the Pinnace fired at a few Indians on
the Beach and killed one of them on which the rest immediately fled
& left the Place clear. To have come away at such a time as this &
forsaken the body of Captn Cook cannot be thought on without
feeling the keenest anguish and Indignation; the Men it must be said
were most sincerely affected on this Occasion & had they been left to
themselves would most certainly have brought him off, when they
came along side they cryed out with Tears in their Eyes that they had
lost their Father![1]

The opportunity to recover the bodies was lost. The main reason for
this terrible oversight was that everybody was in a state of shock.
There was nobody to shout the orders. The corpse of the great
explorer James Cook was left to decay on the beach with those of the
four marines who died with him. Soon afterwards the Hawaiians came
back to find the bodies still lying where they fell and they took the
bodies away to a remote part of the island.

The next move was plain enough. Charles Clerke had been second
in command to Captain Cook. He was now the first in command. It
was a terrible and heavy burden to be shouldered by any man and especially one who was suffering from the illnesses of Charles Clerk, but
the expedition had to soldier on and the responsibility of leadership
fell upon his shoulders. Clerke was a good commander and he knew his
duty. He held a council of war on board the *Resolution*. The suggestion
of revenge was discussed but all agreed that there was absolutely
nothing to be gained from a bloody retribution.

It was unbelievable how it had all happened and how the incident
had escalated so quickly. Nobody really understood the cause of the
conflict. It was obvious that the return of the ships was not welcomed
by certain of the chiefs of the island and by some of the priests, but
the displeasure was by no means universal. Chiefs Palea, Terryaboo and
others seemed to be just as friendly and co-operative as ever. James

Cook himself had acted out of character. It was clear that he had not been his normal self for some time and the theft of the cutter had been the last straw for a man who had carried so much responsibility for so long. The killing of Captain Cook was not a premeditated act. If only the muskets had not been used and if only shots had not been fired in the heat of the moment then things might have turned out very differently. If only the iron daggers had not been sold to the Hawaiians then again things might have been very different. If only Williamson had gone in to the beach instead of pulling further out when Cook had given the signal. If only the mast had not given way when it did. If only the repairs to the mast had been completed earlier and they had sailed the previous day. If only the *Resolution* had decided to call at a different island for repairs.

Charles Clerke led a deputation to Chief Terryaboo. He was received very civilly. The body of Cook had been taken from the rock where he fell. The body had been burnt and the flesh had been cut into many pieces. This was the custom of the island. The Hawaiians knew nothing of British customs or they would have been happy to return the body intact. It transpired that Palea, who had seemed very co-operative with the British, was actually a two-faced traitor. It was he who had planned and executed the theft of the large cutter at the very time that he was making a great show of retrieving the stolen tongs and George Vancouver's cap. The boat had not been stolen to be used for its proper function, it had been torn to pieces for the sake of the iron it contained. Another priest, called Kaireekia or Kariopoo, seemed to understand the need of the British and he offered to retrieve a part of the captain's body. It was a pathetic offering which he brought to the ship, a part of Cook's thigh, which he had obtained for the best possible motives at great risk to his personal safety.

He had a bundle under his arm & he was carried down into the Cabbin where he opened it, and presented to us a Spectacle that struck us with Horror; this was a large piece of human flesh, being the whole of the upper part of a Thigh with the bone taken out, it smelled strong, he

told us repeatedly it was the Thigh of Capt. Cook & that he was
carrying it over as a present to Cahoo from Kariopoo, & we supposed
it might be intended as an Offering to their Gods. We asked him if
they eat the flesh of their Enemies, this he strongly denied; we
enquired for his Head & the rest of the body, he told us that the head
was beat to pieces & the body & Limbs burnt & the Bones in the
possession of Kariopoo. Cahoo, who is the head priest & Chief of
Ohekeaw, to whom the Taboo man belongs, does not seem on this
occasion to espouse the Interest of the King but rather to favour us.[2]

Poor Kaireekia was puzzled by the horrified reaction when he
presented the flesh of the dead commander, but he offered to bring
anything else which was within his power to obtain. This time he
returned with a set of bones which he claimed were the remains of
Captain Cook. Most of the bones had been scraped clean, but the flesh
of one hand was preserved with salt. It had a scar running right down
to the wrist between the thumb and the forefinger. The scar provided
positive identification. It was the mark left by the explosion of a
powder horn off the Newfoundland coast in 1764. It was the scar which
Cook had proudly shown to Palea to show that he was a fighting man.
It was indeed the hand of Captain Cook. The chief Eeapo was another
man who wanted peace and forgiveness. He came again to the ships
with peace offerings, he left with the gift of a silk shirt and some
suspected that his real motives were simply to obtain gifts from the
ship whilst it still remained:

Sunday Feby 21st This Morning Eeapo came down the Hill attended
by a number of men carrying white flags in their Hands, on which a
boat was sent from the *Resolution* to bring him on board; he brought
with him Captn Cook's Hanger, and the 2 barrels of his Gun taken
asunder & the end of one of them beaten flat intended to be made into
Daggers or small adzes. In a short time after, Ke-owa the King's Son
came down to the Beach & was carryed on board the Ship, from
whence he came in the afternoon with Eeapo to the *Discovery*. They tell

us that they are all sorry for what has happened & that they wish to be at peace with us, and that the King is desirous of being our friend again, for which Reason he has sent Eeapo & his son to us; however nothing is more evident than that Kariopoo's chief motive is to get what he can from us before we go away, for his Son did nothing but beg all the time he was with us, & Eeapo found means to return ashore loaded with Presents — among other things he had a silk Shirt given to him which was got from the Russians at Samgoonoodha.[3]

Captain Cook's jawbone was returned, also his feet, one of his shoes and a part of his hat. It had to be accepted these were all the remains that could be recovered. They were put in a coffin and wrapped with the union flag. The flags on both ships were flown at half mast. The yards were crossed. The remains of Captain Cook were given a ceremonial burial at sea with full military honours. The islanders heard the boom of ten four-pounders sounding out across the bay once more but they did not understand the reason. It was a salute to the ship's deceased commander. There was a simple service on deck. At ten minutes to six on Sunday 21 February officers and seamen stood bareheaded in silence, on the decks of the *Resolution* and *Discovery*. Each man had his own set of private memories as the remains of Captain Cook were deposited in the waters of Kealakekua Bay. A few Hawaiians were present. They wept and they asked when their god would return to them again

The repairs to the troublesome mast were completed on the deck of the ship. The next day the ships left Kealakekua Bay for the second time. This time Charles Clerke was in command of the *Resolution* and James King was in command of the *Discovery*. The convoy sailed along the Hawaiian archipelago to the islands of Lanai, Molokai and Oahu. They stopped at Kauai for fresh water and on 1 March they landed at the anchorage on Atiu where the ships had watered in the previous year. Salted pork was in good supply but the yams were out of season. The *Resolution* was still suffering from the leak in her buttocks. The goats, which Cook had left on the island of Niihau the previous year, had perished some time before.

At the end of March Clerke gave orders to leave Hawaii and to haul northwards to Asia, to the Kamchatka Peninsula. It meant crossing the uncharted waters of this part of the Pacific. Clerke knew the orders from the admiralty and he knew his instructions. He also knew that he would die before his duty was completed. Captain Cook was dead, but the expedition was still a voyage of discovery, the seas they were crossing were unknown waters and could contain unknown islands. But no islands were seen and no new discoveries were made. Just as in the previous year, the tropical paradise was left behind and it quickly became much colder. It was amazing how short a time it took to sail from the heat of the tropics to the bitter cold of Siberia. Some of the men had traded their shirts for sexual favours at Hawaii and it was fortunate for them that warm jackets had been stored away in the hold and that they had not been used as items of trade. There was a minor consolation in that there was no shortage of food.

On 19 April the ships were approaching the Russian coastline, the temperature was recorded as 29.5°, a fall of 53° (Fahrenheit) in less than three weeks. They found the village of Petropavlovsk with relative ease, it was the place recommended by the Russian Erasmin Ismylof who had supplied them with letters of introduction from their meeting in Unalaska. The entrance to the harbour was difficult to negotiate because of the ice and there was a minor panic when the Kendall chronometer stopped. The chronometer was by no means worn out, it merely needed an overhaul. Benjamin Lyon, who was a watchmaker by trade, found traces of dirt in the movement and he managed to get it going again.

Clerke's men found that they had landed amongst a miserable habitation of log huts in a snow-covered wilderness — there had been a recent smallpox epidemic that had wiped out much of the population and many of those who remained were suffering from the scurvy. Petropavlovsk was no more than a remote Russian trading outpost and there followed an enforced wait whilst Clerke sent King, Webber and Gore to the authorities at Bolsheretsk, the seat of government and office, which lay on the other side of the peninsula. Clerke knew that it was diplomatically necessary to obtain permission to explore the Russian coastline around the Bering Straits. It took the party two weeks to make the return journey but when they returned it was with the necessary permission.

The British were able to help the Russians with the problem of scurvy by supplying fresh food, the Russians were generous in return and they provided supplies without asking for payment. An interesting item of news was that the people in Petropavlovsk already knew of Cook's visit to the Chukchi tribe in the previous year. The Chukchi had naturally enough assumed that Cook was a Russian and because of his respectable treatment of them they had become far more co-operative when trading with the real Russians.

The stay at Petropavlovsk lasted until June, by which time the ice had retreated and the departure from the harbour was a far easier passage than the arrival. In spite of the atrocious state of the two leaking ships and of the ropes and rigging Clerke set sail again for the Bering Straits and the Arctic Circle. The two ships passed through the Bering Straits without incident and Clerke persisted in his search to the north and west until 19 July. He reached a latitude of 70° 33', it was a little short of Cook's effort in the previous year. There was no way through the ice — in fact it seemed more extensive and harder than the previous year, one reason may have been that it was earlier in the summer.

Clerke continued to carry out his instructions in an exemplary fashion but no new discoveries were made. It was bitterly cold inside the Arctic Circle. It was eerie, desolate and miserable. The two battered and leaky ships, with their torn and patched sails, hobbled around the ice edge of the Arctic Ocean. There was no passage to the east. There was no passage to the north. There was no passage to the west. Even if James Cook had still been in command there would have been no miracle. The ice stood as firm as a stone wall. They could find no passage through or around it. They turned again to the south. On 10 August Charles Clerke dictated a moving letter to his friend Joseph

Banks. Clerke was too weak to write it himself so it was written by James King. It is a moving letter and is quoted in full. It will be remembered that Charles Clerke had been detained in prison just before he left England:

My ever honoured friend,

The disorder I was attacked with in the King's bench prison has proved consumptive, with which I have battled with various success, although without one single days health since I took leave of you in Burlington street; it has now so far got the better of me, that I am not able to turn myself in my bed, so that my stay in this world must be of very short duration; however I hope my friends will have no occasion to blush in owning themselves such, for I have most perfectly & justly done my duty to my country as far as my abilities would enable me, for where that has been concerned, the attention to my health which I was very sensible was in the most imminent danger has never swerved me a single half mile out of the road of my duty; so that I flatter myself I shall leave behind that character it has ever been my utmost ambition to attain, which is that of an honest & faithful servant to the Public whom I had undertaken to serve.

I have made you the best collections of all kinds of matter I could that have fallen in our way in the course of the voyage, but they are by no means so compleat as they would have been had my health enabled me to pay more attention to them; I hope however you will find many among them worthy your attention and acceptance, in my will I have bequeathed you the whole of every kind, there are great abundance so that you will have ample choice.

I must beg you to present my warmest & most affectionate compliments to Dr Solander & assure him I leave the world replete with the most social Ideas of his much esteemed & ever respected Friendship.

I must beg leave to recommend to your notice Mr Will. Ellis one of the Surgeon's mates who will furnish you with some drawings & accounts of the various birds which will come to your possession, he has been very useful to me in your service in that particular, & is I

beleive a very worthy young man & I hope will prove worthy of any
services that may be in your way to confer upon him...

Now my dear & honoured friend I must bid you a final adieu; may
you enjoy many happy years in this world, & in the end attain that
fame your indefatigable industry so richly deserves. These are most
sincerely the warmest and sincerest wishes of your devoted affectionate & departing servant.

Charles Clerke[4]

On 15 August Clerke resigned his command. A week later he died.
Nobody, not even James Cook, had done his duty more than Charles
Clerke. The command of the ships had to be rearranged again. John
Gore, as the senior lieutenant, was now in charge of the ill-fated expedition and James King was promoted to commander of the *Discovery*,
James Burney was promoted to first lieutenant of the *Resolution*. Two
days later the ships were back at Petropavlovsk in the height of the
summer — after the weeks spent in the Arctic seas the little outpost
was a transformed place, the ice had gone and the fields were green.

The time had come at last when they could make for home, but the
return journey was still a voyage to the other side of the world. John
Gore took the ships along the coast of Japan and China into the South
China Sea, still in the hope of discovering new islands but again with
no success. Supplies and fresh meat were found at Pulo Condore where
the local dealers were prepared to give a good price for the Alaskan
furs. When the new year of 1780 arrived the ships were sailing south
from the Chinese mainland. Gore wanted to avoid Batavia because he
had not forgotten the terrible experience with *Endeavour* when nearly
forty men had died on the passage across the Indian Ocean. But he had
to pass very near the island of Java for the only practical route was
through the Straits of Sunda.

There followed the long crossing of the Indian Ocean where John
Gore and a few other veterans of Cook's first great voyage had to live
with the memories of lost friends from the *Endeavour*. The two ships
sailed on. When at last they approached the Cape of Good Hope the

Resolution was so unseaworthy that she could no longer respond to her rudder. Gore dared not risk his ship in the rough seas around the cape and he had to put in at False Bay, Simonstown for repairs. The return to civilisation brought bad news. The American colonists were still fighting for independence and their efforts were supported by the French and the Spanish. The British had come off worst in the latest exchanges. There was a small crumb of comfort. As a scientific expedition of discovery Cook's ships were given diplomatic immunity and they were safe from attack. In a letter dated 10 March 1779 Benjamin Franklin addressed all the captains and commanders of American ships:

Gentlemen,

A Ship having been fitted out from England, before the Commencement of this War, to make Discoveries of new Countries in unknown Seas, under the Conduct of that most celebrated Navigator and Discoverer Captain Cook; an Undertaking truely laudable in itself, as the Increase of Geographical Knowledge facilitates the Communication between distant Nations, in the Exchange of useful Products and Manufactures, and the Extention of Arts, whereby the common Enjoyments of human life are multiply'd and augmented, and Science of other kinds encreased to the Benefit of Mankind in general. This is therefore most earnestly to recommend to every one of you, that in Case the said Ship, which is now expected to be soon in the European Seas on her Return, should happen to fall into your Hands, you would not consider her as an Enemy, nor suffer any Plunder to be made of the Effects contain'd in her, nor obstruct her immediate Return to England, by detaining her or sending her into any other Part of Europe or to America, but that you would treat the said Captain Cook and his People with all Civility and Kindness, affording them as common Friends to Mankind all the Assistance in your Power which they may happen to stand in need of. In so doing you will not only gratify the Generosity of your own Dispositions, But there is no Doubt of your obtaining the Approbation of the Congress and your own American Owners. I have the honour to be . . .

B. Franklin,
Minister Plenipotentiary from the Congress of the United States at
the Court of France[5]

This at least was good news and it guaranteed a safe passage to
England, but there was a drawback. It meant the ships could not travel
with a British squadron for if the squadron were to be attacked then
there was no way the *Resolution* and *Discovery* could stand aside and do
nothing to help. They had to travel the last leg on their own or run the
risk of attack from American, French or Spanish ships.

At Cape Town the journals and other documents were sent ahead
by the merchant ship *Sybil*. The voyage had already stretched out to
four years and there was still the long voyage of several months from
Cape Town to England, but the details are of minor relevance to the
voyage as a whole. When at last they were back again in the Northern
Hemisphere, they discovered that it was not just the Pacific which
could produce contrary winds. In the middle of July in mid Atlantic,
the ships were blown so far off course by strong easterly winds that
they were carried to the west of Ireland. They were obliged to sail all
the way round the north of Scotland to get home and the first landfall
on British soil was an unheralded stop at the Orkney Islands on 22
August. James King was sent overland to London, probably only as a
precaution for, considering that he had to cross to the Scottish mainland
and travel almost the full length of Scotland and England, it is hard to
believe that he would arrive in London before the ships. The last leg of
the voyage was symbolic in that it followed the east coast of the British
Isles with two weary ships sailing past the Yorkshire ports of Staithes,
Whitby and Hull in Cook's own nursery of the North Sea. On 4
October the *Resolution* arrived at last at the estuary of the Thames.
Samuel Gibson, the marine veteran of all three voyages, had been taken
ill as they passed through the Straits of Sunda. He died on the very last
leg of the journey and he never set foot on English soil again.

News of the death of Captain Cook arrived in England long before them. Whilst they were working their long sea passage across the Indian and Atlantic Oceans the letters from Unalaska and Petropavlovsk had dutifully crossed the whole of Asia by land and were forwarded from Moscow to reach England in January 1780. The *London Gazette* broke the news to the public on 11 January, thus by the time the *Resolution* arrived in October it was all yesterday's news.

It was an emotional homecoming, but it was not accompanied by the official welcomes that Captain Cook had received on his two previous voyages. It was difficult for the nation to know how to receive the explorers except in terms of bereavement and condolences. The whole expedition was surely a failure. Captain Cook was dead. Many other able men such as Charles Clerke and William Anderson had perished on the voyage. Cook's handling of his crew and of the Pacific islanders was not up to the standards of his first two voyages. There was no North West Passage. The main object of the voyage had not been achieved. And yet. When the dust had settled. When the mourning for Captain Cook was over. When there was a degree of perspective on the achievements of the last four years. When the time came to consider the voyage in its right context away from the death of the commander. Only then was it seen that in spite of all the difficulties Captain Cook had in fact achieved a third and final great voyage.

There were new latitudes and new longitudes. There was the landing at Kerguelen, the island of desolation, an island so remote that it was willingly conceded to the French. There was much to add to the maps and the customs of Tonga and Tahiti. After these preliminaries there was the latter part of the voyage when Cook achieved again some of his former greatness. The archipelago of Hawaii was a major discovery, in fact it was the most important discovery in the North Pacific. There was a great slice of luck in the discovery, but we all know that genius makes its own luck. We must not forget the six months of hard graft on the west coast of North America, a pioneering survey which will always be seen as the first major survey of that formidable coast. The mapping and charting of the north west coast of America was certainly not due to luck. It was an arduous six months of sheer hard work and brilliant seamanship. The maps and the charts which the ships brought home were only a preliminary survey, it would have taken at least twice as long to map and chart every island on such a complex coastline. The task was completed fifteen years later by George Vancouver who never failed to voice his appreciation for his former captain.

There was the passage through the Bering Straits and the mapping of the Arctic Ocean that put the boastful maps of Stahlin and Muller into the rubbish bin of history. The North West Passage did not and could not open up to Captain Cook. It belonged to Franklin and Ross and to the great explorers of a later age. But when at long last steam-powered iron ships became available, a passage from Atlantic to Pacific was found, then all concerned acknowledged their debt to those who had gone before and who had braved the perils of the Arctic ice in their frail wooden sailing vessels.

As regards posterity George Vancouver was the most famous of Cook's men but he was by no means the only member of the expedition to achieve distinction. William Bligh was the most notorious. He returned to Tahiti a few years later to collect specimens of the bread fruit, and he is remembered principally on that voyage by the infamous mutiny on the *Bounty*. Bligh's botanist on the *Bounty* was David Nelson, his shipmate on the *Resolution*. David Nelson was set adrift with Bligh after the mutiny and he died in Timor of fever and exposure. Bligh survived the mutiny, he went on to serve under Horatio Nelson and in 1801 he captained the 56-gun *Glatton* at the battle of Copenhagen. In 1808 he became the governor of New South Wales and in 1814 he was promoted to vice-admiral. Edward Riou also saw service at Copenhagen, as commander of the 38-gun *Amazon*, and it was there, much to Nelson's grief, that he lost his life. John Gore was nearer to the end of his distinguished career, he was given Cook's vacant berth at Greenwich and he died there in 1790. James Burney still had a long career ahead of him after Cook's voyages and he rose to become a rear-admiral in 1821. His publications included a massive five-volume work on the discoveries in the Pacific Ocean and on the lighter side he wrote a treatise on the game of whist. Molesworth Phillips, lieutenant of the marines, married Susan Burney the sister of James Burney. According to Fanny Burney Molesworth Phillips did not treat her sister well.

James King had a distinguished academic career, he wrote the third volume of the official account of the voyage. He became a Fellow of the Royal Society in 1782 but he died of consumption two years later in Nice. James Trevenen was appointed by the Russians to command another voyage of exploration in the North Pacific but before he could sail he was called to serve his country in the war against Sweden. 'I remember having seen him take off his coat two or three times in an evening at the Duke of Gloucester's', wrote one of Trevenen's contempories, 'To exhibit to some curious ladies his tattoo'd arms'. John Williamson, who never lived down his misinterpretation of Cook's signal to bring his boat in, rose to become captain of the *Agincourt* but his career ended in 1797 when he was court-martialled for 'unsatisfactory behaviour' after the battle of Camperdown. John Ledyard, the corporal of the marines who made the uncomfortable journey by canoe in Unalaska, was asked to fight for the British against the Americans. He was born in America, he refused to take sides for the second time and it probably cost him his commission. Even the ship's chronometer should be given a mention, it sailed with the first fleet on the colonisation of Australia.

All these men had seen their commander at his best and at his worst after three years as shipmates. Many went on to serve under Nelson and until the Battle of Trafalgar and much later the survivors could still be found occasionally in the dockside taverns of the British sea ports. They were all 'Cook's men'. For the rest of their lives they boasted that they had sailed under Captain Cook. Their eyes glazed over as they spoke of the Pacific Ocean, of New Zealand, and of the bitter cold of the Arctic and Antarctic seas.

When the data for the final voyage came under scrutiny and the journals became available it could not be denied that a third great voyage had been completed. In terms of new discoveries it may have been less than the two previous voyages but it was still a very significant voyage. It was longer in duration than either of the two previous voyages, but above all it was destined to be remembered by posterity as the last voyage of Captain Cook.

And what of Cook's family? We must respect the privacy of Elizabeth Cook who lived another sixty-two years as a sailor's widow! Elizabeth must have asked the question 'why' many times. Why had he given up his comfortable retirement at Greenwich Hospital to voyage again to the distant Pacific and to the inhospitable Arctic? Yet she knew him better than anybody else either before or since. He may not have spent much time at home with her and his family, but he provided for them very adequately and he brought them honour and fame. The rare months between the long voyages, when they had been together, were happy memories. He simply could not rest on his laurels and he was not ready to enjoy his retirement at Greenwich. He wanted to sail the Pacific seas again. He wanted to make new discoveries, he wanted to chart new coasts and he wanted to sail where no ship had sailed before. Perhaps in his heart of hearts he wanted to die in service. He wanted to end his life in his beloved Pacific and his ideal was to be laid to rest in the blue waters of a bay on one of the most beautiful islands in the world, an island for which he himself could claim the discovery.

TWELVE

Aftermath

After a lapse of two centuries we cannot close the story of Captain Cook's final voyage without a review of his life and his achievements. Cook had been close to death many times before the disaster at Kealakekua Bay. In the eighteenth century any sailor who had been at sea for as many years as James Cook was lucky to be still alive to spin his yarns. The fogs and the sandbanks and the treacherous tidal estuaries of the Thames and the Tyne gave the young James Cook many close calls during his merchant navy service as a young man on the North Sea. His early years in the Royal Navy also held some life threatening experiences. The exploding powder horn in Newfoundland could easily have killed him even before he undertook his first great voyage of exploration. When he surveyed the east coast of Australia in the *Endeavour* there were two occasions when he came very close to a watery grave. The first time was when the ship struck the hidden coral of the Great Barrier Reef, it could not be refloated for twenty-four hours, but the *Endeavour* and her crew were saved by good fortune and brilliant seamanship. Only a few months later on the same voyage, the *Endeavour* was almost carried onto a wall of sharp coral by the rushing tide. This time it was not brilliant seamanship that saved the ship, it was providence which sent a mere breath of wind at the last minute to carry her away from certain death. Later on the same voyage came the terrible crossing of the Indian Ocean when many of the crew of the *Endeavour* died from dysentery and malaria.

On his second voyage Cook made a foray to 71° south in the bitter cold of the Antarctic. Could any other ship have taken such a risk and come back to tell the tale? On the same voyage there was a confrontation at the island of Eromanga in the New Hebrides, it was an incident that could easily have turned into a disaster like that of Kealakekua Bay. There were many other lesser-known dangers such as when the *Resolution* was caught in the shoal water off the coast of New Caledonia, and we must not forget the murder of twelve seamen from Furneaux's ship the *Adventure* at Grass Cove in New Zealand.

On the third voyage there was a plot to capture the ships at the Tonga Isles, and there were close scrapes with the warlike Maoris on all Cook's visits to New Zealand. His approaches to the indigenous peoples of the Pacific were always peaceful and calculated, but by the time he reached Hawaii on his final voyage he was tired and irritated by the responsibility of too many years in office. He did not handle the situation with his usual tact and diplomacy.

In Cook's time we witness the great advances in navigation and exploration and we find the world map redrawn after each of his three great voyages. In 1768, when Cook first entered the Pacific Ocean from around Cape Horn, little had been added to the geography of the Pacific since the pioneering voyages of the sixteenth and seventeenth centuries. At the time of Cook's death however, the map of the Pacific was far more complete. The whole of New Zealand had been added to the world map by the voyage of the *Endeavour* and also much of Australia, even though the latter still had many miles of uncharted coast. Cook's second voyage did not include any large new landmasses, he did all in his power to discover the southern continent which was Antarctica, but in a wooden sailing ship powered only by the wind it was an impossible quest in the freezing latitudes of the deep south. Many more islands were added to the map however, complete with their correct latitude and longitude. Cook was fortunate to be the first explorer to enjoy the benefits of a ship's chronometer, which made him into the first navigator of an era when longitudes could be calculated with a high degree of confidence. In summing up his achievements we must not forget his meticulous attention to other details of long voyages. He was able almost to eradicate the problem of scurvy on his ships, partly because of the diet which he attended to very carefully and to the constant search for fresh food, but it was also due to the health and cleanliness of the ship both inside and out.

It was inevitable that the accounts of the voyages, the paintings and the artefacts of the South Seas and the appearance in Europe of individuals from the Pacific Islands would create a lasting impression on society. There was great rivalry between the British and the French claims for priority. Bougainville was at Tahiti before Cook's first visit, but Wallis with his ship the *Dolphin* landed there the year before Bougainville. It was the Frenchman Bougainville who introduced the first Tahitian into European society, but the British were not to be outdone and the Tahitian Omai arrived in London in 1774. The appearance of Omai in London society was almost an accident. He did not arrive with Cook, he arrived in England on the *Adventure*, captained by Cook's second in command Tobias Furneaux. On his second voyage Cook's two ships lost contact with each other after a violent storm off the coast of New Zealand and they were unable to keep a rendezvous. If the *Adventure* had managed to remain in contact with the *Resolution* then Cook would probably have returned Omai to his own people, for he had great reservations about taking men out of their own environment into a strange new world. Odiddy, the Tahitian who travelled with Cook to the Antarctic on the *Resolution*, was returned to his own people only a few months later. Omai did arrive in England however, and he turned out to be a great success in London society. He had the right personality to learn English manners and to mix well with society. The gossip mongers of the day, such as Johnson's biographer James Boswell and Fanny Burney the sister of Cook's lieutenant James Burney, spoke very highly of Omai and during his stay in England he did much to promote the idea of the noble savage. The latter was a question very much debated in eighteenth-century society. Was the society of the South Seas every bit as good as that of Europe even though they did not have the advantage of the history, the science, the literature, the technology and all the other things which were assumed to be part of a civilised society?

In Paris Rousseau published his *Discours sur les arts et Sciences* in 1749, this was two decades before the voyages of Cook and Bougainville. It was he who introduced the concept of the noble savage, a simple and unsophisticated people living in an Arcadia where the complexities, vices and poverty of the 'civilised' European world did not exist. When the explorers returned with accounts of Tahiti, a land of perpetual sunshine where the bread grew on trees, where free love was practised and offered to all new arrivals, it seemed that the paradise of the noble savage existed in the Pacific Ocean. It was Diderot, the friend of Rousseau, who developed the idea of the noble savage further in the supplement to the published account of Bougainville's voyage. The question was, did European society have any right to interfere with the society of the noble savage?

The Romantic age in Europe was approaching very rapidly, the first of the Romantic poets were alive even though the bulk of their poetry was still a generation away from publication. It was not surprising that the thoughts of the Romantic school were influenced by the idea of a utopia in the Southern Hemisphere but those Europeans, such as Joseph Banks and Daniel Solander, who had actually been to Tahiti knew that the truth was not as simple as it was usually presented. They knew that there were frequent civil wars on Tahiti, there were wide class distinctions, there was no legal system to speak of, there was infanticide and human sacrifice and the Tahitians had never heard of the eighth commandment 'Thou shalt not steal'.

There is something of a paradox in these enlightened views of the rights of the noble savage. This was the age when the transatlantic slave trade had reached its height. Almost every day ships were leaving England from London, Bristol and Liverpool for the coast of Africa. Each vessel carried hundreds of black Africans, held in chains between the decks in atrocious cramped conditions, torn from their homes and families to be sold across the Atlantic into slavery on the sugar and tobacco plantations of America. It was also the time of the American Revolution. The French Revolution, only a few years behind America, was waiting to explode only a decade after the death of Cook. Amongst the cries for liberty and freedom it was Samuel Johnson who coined the phrase 'how is it that we hear the loudest yelps for liberty amongst the drivers of Negroes?' Those who respected the rights of the noble savage were the same enlightened people as those who started the movement for the abolition of slavery. The Abolitionists won their case after many years of struggle, but it was not until the nineteenth century that the slave trade was abolished and there was nothing they could do to prevent the exploitation of the Pacific Ocean and its people.

The British, the French and the Spanish all made their territorial claims to Tahiti and the Society Islands. Tahiti was so well situated in the middle of the southern Pacific that it was no wonder it became so popular. The fact that it was a watering place and a source of fresh food and reprovisioning was in itself a reason for spending time at Tahiti. Add to that the open welcome of the people plus the sexual attraction and the loose morals of the islands and it was impossible for any captain to cross the Pacific without spending time there. In the early days the Society Islands benefited a little from the trade and the contact, but as time progressed it was inevitable that the trade turned into exploitation. The trading of metal cooking utensils and of manu-factured cloth eventually led to the loss of traditional skills of cloth making and pottery on the islands themselves. Cook himself recog-nised that this could become a problem and on his last visit to Tahiti he recorded his feelings in his journal. He claimed that in a single decade the use of iron tools had caused them to abandon their tradi-tional tools of stone and bone:

> I cannot avoid expressing it as my real opinion that it would have been far better for these poor people never to have known our superiority in the accommodations and arts that make life comfortable, than after

once knowing it, to be again left and abandoned in their original inca-pacity of improvement. Indeed they cannot be restored to that happy mediocrity in which they lived before we discovered them, if the inter-course between us should be discontinued. It seems to me that it has become, in a manner, incumbent on the Europeans to visit them once in three or four years, in order to supply them with those conveniences which we have introduced among them, and have given them a predilection for. The want of such occasional supplies will, probably, be felt very heavily by them, when it may be too late to go back to their old, less perfect, contrivances, which they now despise, and have discontinued since the introduction of ours. For, by the time that the iron tools, of which they are now possessed, are worn out, they will have almost lost the knowledge of their own. A stone hatchet is, at present, as rare a thing amongst them, as an iron one was eight years ago, and a chisel of bone or stone is not to be seen.[1]

By the nineteenth century whaling vessels from the American ports of Nantucket and New Bedford made Tahiti their regular port of call. They traded with cheap liquor and alcohol. Tahiti became a place full of vice, drunkenness and prostitution. There was a happier moral influx, which did much to improve the situation, with the coming of the London Missionary Society late in the eighteenth century. The missionaries knew about the shortcomings of Tahitian society, they knew about the human sacrifices, the infanticide and the frequent civil wars. They believed that the answer to these problems was to convert the island to Christianity. At first the Tahitians were totally confused by the religious ideals from another culture but the missionaries stuck to their task with great zeal and by the first decade of the nineteenth century much of the island had been converted. What the Missionary Society did not appreciate was that by changing to a European lifestyle they were systematically destroying much of the local culture. The island dancing for example, was suppressed as being far too lewd and offensive for European taste. The situation bore some resemblance to the state of England after the civil war when the Puritans were in

power and any form of enjoyment was frowned upon. Later in the nineteenth century, when the full prudery of Victorian religion reached its
apogee, the island traditions were suppressed even further.

It is an unfortunate fact that no account of the Society Islands and
the South Pacific can be complete without some mention of the
problem of venereal disease. Cook, Bougainville and other captains
from the early days of the European contact all vehemently denied that
they were responsible for the introduction of the disease to the Pacific
Islands. Certainly all the responsible captains took elaborate precautions to prevent the spread of the disease, but Cook could never be
quite sure whether or not his men were responsible for some of the
outbreaks which inevitably occurred. With so many journals and
detailed accounts of his voyages it is easy enough to find instances
where the disease seems to be attributed to one of Cook's ships. The
problem is complicated however, by the endemic disease of yaws which
was present in the islands long before the contact with Europe; the
loose layman's descriptions in the journals are not detailed enough to
differentiate between the two. Even when Cook specifically banned
the Tahitian women from his ships the eagerness of the girls and of the
European men made it impossible to keep them apart. Both Cook and
Bougainville took as many precautions as seemed reasonable at the
time to prevent the spread of the disease, but it was impossible to stop
it entirely.

The subsequent development and settlement of Australia and New
Zealand came later than in the Society Islands. These countries were
so large that the first settlers affected only a small part, in the case of
Australia around the convict settlement at Botany Bay. For two or
three generations the aboriginal had been able to ignore the white
settlers. Conflict between settlers and aboriginals was common but it
was confined to the area around Botany Bay and Port Jackson. The
potential of the new country was very obvious however, and it was
ridiculous to use a natural resource as large as the east coast of
Australia as a penal colony. The permanent settlers and farmers soon
followed the convicts. The fact that the new settlers brought trade and

prosperity with them meant that new forms of wealth and opportunity came the way of the aboriginal. This was at the expense of destroying a way of life which had existed for millennia and the insensitive treatment of the aboriginal was bound to lead to eventual conflict. The situation bears some resemblance to the abysmal treatment of the native peoples of America, where the Indian tribes were successively driven off their lands and hunting grounds into ever shrinking reservations. In Australia, as the number of new arrivals continued to increase, the settlers claimed the fertile land for farming, and the same arguments were put forward for the productive use of the land. The aboriginals were a nomadic people with no permanent settlements or residences, they had no legal body to fight their prior claim to the land.

The settlement of New Zealand came later. It was felt that something had to be done about the indigenous population. The Maoris were a proud race of warriors but one custom the settlers wanted to rid them of was their taste for cannibalism. As with Tahiti, there was continual conflict between the different Maori tribes. In 1773 when Cook landed at Dusky Sound on the South Island he made contact with some of the last survivors of the local tribe who were hunted down and killed by the more numerous and powerful Maoris around the Cook Strait. War between the conflicting Maori tribes was common and this fact was used as an excuse to deprive them of their land. Tasman lost men on his first landing at Murderers Bay, Cook lost twelve men from the *Adventure* on his second voyage, and the Frenchman Marion du Fresne was killed with fourteen of his men in New Zealand. His lieutenant Julien Crozet wrote what was the general European view of the Maoris in his century:

> I contend that among all created animals there is nothing more savage and dangerous than the natural and savage peoples themselves... I endeavored to stimulate their curiosity, to learn the emotions that could be awakened in their souls, but found nothing but vicious tendencies among these children of nature; and they are all the more

dangerous in that they greatly surpass Europeans in physical strength. Within the same quarter of an hour I have found them to change from childish delight to deepest gloom, from complete calmness to the greatest heights of rage, and then burst into immoderate laughter the moment afterwards. I have noticed them change towards each other, one moment caressing, and menacing the next; but they were never long in the same mood, and always struck me as having dangerous and deceitful tendencies.[2]

The exploitation of the Pacific people by the European nations is a fact which has to be accepted. The question here is to what degree do we lay the blame on James Cook? After Cook's third great voyage of exploration the Pacific Ocean was no longer an unknown quantity. There were still a few islands waiting to be discovered and there were some whose positions were not accurately recorded. There were still many questions of language, tradition and anthropology that remained unanswered. The Pacific was charted however. The ship's chronometer was still an expensive and rare instrument but it was only a question of time before it became readily available to all nations. These factors meant that the Pacific Islands were accessible to any ship and any nation that wished to go there. The Pacific had been opened up by Captain Cook and others. It was ripe for exploitation.

This was not the way Cook viewed the situation. He saw himself as an explorer and a discoverer. He wanted to produce maps and charts of the unknown parts of the world for others to use and follow him. His journals show that he had a great interest in the life and customs of the Pacific, they are accurate and objective and they are an invaluable record of a world which was changing rapidly and which could not be recreated. He exploited the people to the extent that he wanted to supply his ship and his crew. He bartered nails, beads, mirrors and manufactured items in exchange for food and supplies. He also bartered to obtain ornaments and artefacts of the Pacific Islands to bring back to Europe. He always took great care to respect local customs, to discover the ruler of the island and to find out who owned the property. He even took the trouble to ask permission where he thought it was relevant, to cut down trees to supply masts and timbers for his ships. His respect for the native traditions was always exemplary. It was rare for him to record his feelings and emotions about individuals but there is no doubt that he enjoyed the Pacific islanders and there is no doubt that they in turn had a great respect for him. There were many times when he bartered a few nails for an island pig or for a large quantity of fruit and vegetables, but this was out of the necessity of feeding his men with fresh meat and food for their sustenance and his continual precautions to keep scurvy at bay.

To blame Cook for the exploitation of the Pacific is equivalent to blaming Albert Einstein for the atomic bomb. The scientist, in his search for the truth about the laws of nature and the structure of the atom, discovered the relationship between matter and energy and so proved the possibility of making atomic weapons by the release of large quantities of energy. The atomic bomb was not the quest of the scientist, he was searching only for truth and he accidentally stumbled on the discovery that the bomb was possible. Exactly the same is true of Cook. His orders were to search for new lands in the Southern Hemisphere. His voyages were quests of discovery, to seek out the facts of the unknown world and to add new knowledge about geography, anthropology, botany, zoology and many other sciences. The result of his work made the Pacific far more accessible to exploitation. Without Cook's contribution to the world map the exploitation of the Pacific would have been much later, perhaps by twenty or thirty years, but the eventual outcome would have been very little different.

Many writers complain about our lack of knowledge of Cook's character. He wrote millions of words of which many are dry and routine reports of latitudes, longitudes and weather, with no reference to his feelings and emotions. When he comes to describe his discoveries, the geography and the anthropology of the places he visits then we have accurate scientific descriptions but again we learn nothing of Cook's own feelings and emotions. The criticisms are sometimes unfair, it was his duty to report his findings as factually and accurately as he could and he was always very careful to stick slavishly to the admiralty guidelines. Everything he wrote would be read and scrutinised by his superiors at the admiralty and he could be called to account for any of his actions. There is little doubt that there are instances when his journals and his log play down very dangerous situations and poor seamanship in case the blame for failure could be laid at his door. The journals of his other officers are more relaxed and emotional than those of Captain Cook. The journals of Joseph Banks and even John Rienhold Forster are more emotional and contain details which Cook does not give, but they were not bound by the same restrictions as the captain of the ship. In spite of all his devotion to fact the character of James Cook does appear in his writings. The journals do describe the man whom other people saw. The steady, unemotional, impassive man who ruled the ship with scrupulous fairness and with a rod of iron.

There are some instances where he does give vent to his feelings, one example is on the voyage of the *Endeavour* when he finally left behind the treacherous coast of Australia after two near disasters on the Great Barrier Reef. He muses on the life of an explorer:

Was it not for the pleasure which Naturly results to a man from his being the first discoverer even was it nothing more than Sand or Shoals this kind of service would be unsupportable especially in far distant parts like this, Short of Provisions & almost every other necessary. People will hardly admit of an excuse for a man leaving a coast unexplored he has once discov'd, if dangers are his excuse he is then charged with Timerousness & want of Perseverance, & at once pronounced the most unfit man in the world to be employ'd as a discoverer, if on the other hand he boldly encounters all the dangers and Obstacles he meets with & is unfortunate enough not to succed he is charged with Temerity & Perhaps want of Conduct the former of the Aspersions I am confident can never be laid to my Charge, & if I am fortunate to surmount all the Dangers we meet with the latter will never be brot in question, altho' I must own that I have engaged more among the Islands & shoals upon this coast then perhaps in Prudence I ought to have done with a single Ship, & every other thing considered but if I had not I should not have been able to give any better account of the one half of it, than if I had never seen it, at best I should not have been able to say wether it was Main land or Islands & as to its produce, that we should have been totally ignorant of as being inseparable with the other & in this case it would have been far more satisfaction to me never to have discov'd it, but it is time I should have done with this Subject wch at best is but disagreeable & which I was lead into on reflecting on our late Danger.[3]

Another example is when he penetrated to over 71° south on his second voyage and he was forced to turn the ship to the north when he met with a frozen sea of solid ice. 'I who had Ambition not only to go farther than any one had done before, but as far as it was possible for man to go.' He would doubtless have sailed on to the South Pole if the sea had allowed him to do so:

I will not say it was impossible any where to get farther to the South, but the attempting it would have been a dangerous and rash enterprise and what I believe no man in my situation would have thought of. It was indeed my opinion as well as the opinion of most on board, that this Ice extended quite to the Pole or perhaps joins to some land, to which it had been fixed from the creation and that it here, that is to the South of this Parallel, where all the Ice we find scatered up and down to the North are first form'd and afterwards broke off by gales of Wind or other cause and brought to the North by the Currents which we have always found to set in that direction in the high Latitudes. As we drew near this Ice some Penguins were heard but none seen and but few other birds or any other thing that could induce us to think any land was near; indeed if there was any land behind this Ice it could afford no better retreat for birds or any other animals, than the Ice it self, with which it must have been wholy covered. I who had Ambition not only to go farther than any one had done before, but as far as it was possible for man to go, was not sorry at meeting with this interruption as it in some measure relieved us, at least shortned the dangers and hardships inseparable with the Navigation of the Southern Polar Rigions; Sence therefore, we could not proceed one Inch farther to the South, no other reason need be assigned for my Tacking and Standing back to the north, being at this time in the Latitude of 71° 10' S, Longitude 106° 54' W. It was happy for us that the Weather was Clear when we fell in with this Ice and that we discovered it so soon as we did for we had no sooner Tacked then we were involved in a thick fog. The Wind was at East and blew a fresh breeze, so that we were inabled to return back over that space we had already made our selves acquainted with. At Noon the Mercury in the Thermometer stood at 32½ ° [Fahrenheit] and we found the air exceeding cold.[4]

The character of James Cook comes through to us through his journals and his writings. He shared the confined space of a crowded ship with a hundred or more seamen. It is true that as captain he had more space and privacy than any other man on the ship, but the captain's cabin was not a place where he could relax and enjoy some privacy, it was the place where all the problems of the ship were brought for him to solve. In spite of this he remained a silent and unapproachable man. He was not one to share his thoughts and his ideas with his officers. It was a fault and they frequently complained that they were not told where they were going or what was to happen next on the voyage. But this was James Cook and this was his character, the strong silent man. He was always calculating odds and taking risks where they could be justified but seldom trusting to the judgement of his officers. His officers too knew his character well and would defend him always during his lifetime and after his death.

It is no longer possible for any ship to cross the Pacific Ocean without encountering the ghost of Captain Cook. It is not possible to sail around the world without criss-crossing Cook's path many times. Captain Cook's voyages have become the story of maritime legend, circumnavigators sailing around the world under sail expect that at any time the ghost of *Endeavour* or the *Resolution* may appear in the middle of the night in the watery empty loneliness of the vast Pacific Ocean.

The boy who was born the son of an obscure farm labourer became the greatest navigator of his age, he became the greatest navigator of all time. Wherever the white surf breaks on the Pacific Islands there are memories of James Cook. Wherever the North Sea breaks against the east coast we remember a younger James Cook. At Whitby, at Hull, at the seaports of East Anglia, on the treacherous sandbanks which guard the entrance to the River Thames we see his training ground, but most of all on the weather-beaten coast of north Yorkshire. Go to Staithes where the young Cook was an apprentice in a long-lost grocer's shop near the sea front. This is where the lad first saw the fishing smacks arriving in the harbour and where he saw greater ships pass by with their cargoes for distant parts. He watched the sea breaking on the cold grey pebbles of the North Sea, and he longed to sail that sea which he knew encompassed the whole earth. Alfred Lord Tennyson found a form of words to express his feelings:

> Break, break, break
> On thy cold grey stones, O Sea!
> And I would that my tongue could utter
> The thoughts that arise in me.
>
> O well for the fisherman's boy,
> That he shouts with his sister at play!
> O well for the sailor lad,
> That he sings in his boat on the bay!
>
> And the stately ships go on
> To their haven under the hill;
> But O for the touch of a vanish'd hand
> And the sound of a voice that is still!

Break, break, break,
At the foot of thy crags O Sea!
But the tender grace of a day that is dead
Will never come back to me.

Alfred, Lord Tennyson (1809-1892)

References

Beaglehole III:
  Beaglehole, J C: *The Journals of Captain James Cook*
  Vol III, *The voyage of the Resolution and Discovery 1776-1780*,
  Published for the Hakluyt Society, Cambridge 1967

This book is the main source of information for the voyage, giving extracts from many original journals. They are referenced as follows:

Anderson: pp 723-986
Burney, James : pp697-701, 1340-1342
Clerke : pp 531-549, 569-582, 591-603,632-650, 655-659, 678-697,
    1301-1340
Cook : pp 1- 491
Edgar: pp 701-709, 1351-1360
Gilbert: pp 709-718
King : pp 495-531, 549-569, 582-591, 603-632, 650-654, 659-678, 1361-
    1454
Samwell: pp 987-1300
Williamson: pp1342-1351

Other references are:

Beaglehole I:
  Beaglehole, J C: *The Journals of Captain James Cook Vol I,*
  The voyage of the Endeavour 1768-1771,
  Published for the Hakluyt Society, Cambridge 1955
Beaglehole II:
  Beaglehole, J C: *The Journals of Captain James Cook*
  Vol II, *The voyage of the Resolution and Adventure 1772-1775,*
  Published for the Hakluyt Society, Cambridge 1961
Beaglehole IV:
  Beaglehole, J C: *The Life of Captain James Cook*
  The Journals of Captain James Cook Vol IV, The Hakluyt Society,
  London 1974
Boswell, J.
  The Life of Samuel Johnson LL D, London 1927
Charles Burney:
  Alvaro Ribeiro, S J (Ed): *The Letters of Dr Charles Burney Vol I*
  1751-1784, Oxford 1991
Fanny Burney Vol II:
  Lars E Troide (Ed): *The Early Journals and letters of Fanny Burney*
  Vol II 1774-1777 Oxford 1990
Fanny Burney Vol III:
  Lars E Troide and Stewart J Cooke (Eds): *The Early Journals and*
  letters of Fanny Burney Vol III 1778-1779 Oxford 1994
Moorhead, Alan
  The Fatal Impact, London 1966
Percy A Scholes (Ed)
  The Great Dr Burney, Oxford 1948
Kippis, Andrew
  The Life of Captain James Cook, London 1788
Vancouver, George
  A Voyage of Discovery to the North Pacific Ocean and round the
  World. (3 vols), London 1798

Notes

Chapter One

1　Beaglehole IV p. 445
2　Boswell ii pp. 5-6
3　Fanny Burney Vol II p. 62
4　Fanny Burney Vol II p. 41
5　Fanny Burney Vol II p. 60
6　Boswell ii p. 6
7　Kippis pp. 324-5
8　Beaglehole IV p. 474

Chapter Two

1　Fanny Burney Vol II p. 104
2　Fanny Burney Vol II p. 206
3　Beaglehole IV p. 507

Chapter Three

1　Beaglehole III p. 14
2　Anderson p. 736
3　Anderson p. 743
4　Liverpool Public Library,
　　Gregson Correspondence,

XVII., Beaglehole III pp1514-15

5　ibid
6　ibid
7　Anderson p. 757
8　Beaglehole IV p. 511

Chapter Four

1　Anderson p. 770
2　Anderson p. 771
3　Anderson p. 785
4　Anderson pp. 786-7
5　Anderson p. 787
6　Burney: Beaglehole III p. 54 n2
7　Bayly: Beaglehole III p. 53 n2
8　Beaglehole III p. 63
9　Burney: Beaglehole III p. 64 n2
10　Beaglehole III p. 68
11　Beaglehole III p. 68
12　Burney: Beaglehole III p. 66 n1

Chapter Five

1 Burney: Beaglehole III p. 107 n1
2 Burney: Beaglehole III p. 108 n2
3 Anderson p. 875
4 Anderson pp. 875-876
5 Williamson: Beaglehole III p. 110 n3
6 Anderson p. 881
7 Clerke: Beaglehole III p. 122 n2
8 Samwell p. 1042
9 Samwell p. 1030
10 Samwell p. 1049

Chapter Six

1 Martin: Beaglehole III p. 183 n1
2 Bayly, Beaglehole III p. 193 n2
3 Samwell p. 1063
4 Beaglehole III pp. 214-5
5 Beaglehole III p. 212
6 Williamson: Beaglehole III p. 240 n4

Chapter Seven

1 Samwell p. 1081
2 King : Beaglehole III p. 265 n1
3 Clerke: Beaglehole III p. 265 n1
4 Edgar: Beaglehole III p. 266 n1
5 King p. 1393
6 King p. 1394

Chapter Eight

1 Beaglehole III p. 300
2 Trevenen, Beaglehole III p. 303 n2
3 Samwell p.1095

4 Vancouver, Vol III, pp 208-9
5 Beaglehole III p. 350
6 King p. 1421
7 Bayly: Beaglehole III p. 391 n 4
8 Beaglehole III p. 406
9 Beaglehole III p. 410
10 King : Beaglehole III 414 n2
11 Beaglehole III p. 418

Chapter Nine

1 Samwell p. 1138
2 King p. 1445
3 King p. 1446
4 King p. 1454
5 King p. 1455

Chapter Ten

1 Beaglehole III p. 481
2 Samwell p. 1155
3 Beaglehole III p. 479
4 Burney: Beaglehole III p. 490 n 6
5 Beaglehole III p. 491
6 Samwell p. 1173
7 Samwell p. 1164
8 Burney: Beaglehole III p. 490 n 3
9 Burney: Beaglehole III p. 490 n 5
10 Edgar p. 1360
11 Edgar p. 1360
12 Samwell p. 1198

Chapter Eleven

1 Samwell p. 1200
2 Samwell p. 1209
3 Samwell p. 1217

4 Beaglehole III p. 1543

5 Beaglehole III p. 1535

Chapter Twelve

1 Moorhead p. 70

2 Moorhead p. 78

3 Beaglehole I p. 546

4 Beaglehole II p. 323

Index